Screenplays as Literature Series
Dramas
3

NIETZSCHE: A DANGEROUS LIFE

An Historical Biography Movie Script
About History's Most Infamous Atheist

Original Screenplay
by
Brian James Godawa

Story
by
Brian James Godawa
and
Adam Christing

Nietzsche: A Dangerous Life: An Historical Biography Movie Script About History's Most Infamous Atheist
Screenplays as Literature Series • Dramas • 3
1st Edition

Cover images used under license from Shutterstock.com.

Warrior Poet Publishing
www.warriorpoetpublishing.com

ISBN: 978-1-942858-52-2 (paperback)
ISBN: 978-1-942858-53-9 (ebook)

Get this FREE Ebooklet

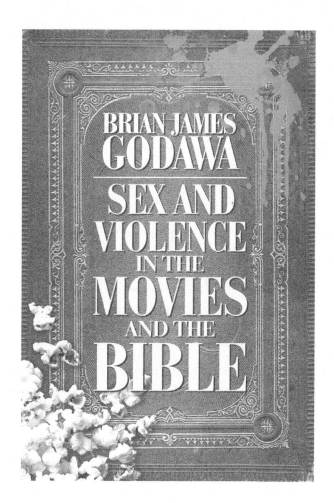

Too Much Sex and Violence in the Movies?

That's what some Christians argue. But just how much is enough? Author Brian Godawa examines the Bible to see how it depicts the sins of humanity accurately without exploitation.

Just click on this link to get your FREE ebooklet:

https://godawa.com/sex-and-violence-ebook/

Table of Contents

How to Read a Screenplay

The essential purpose of a screenplay is to be a blueprint out of which a movie is made. For this reason, screenplays or scripts are technically unfinished "works in progress." Movies are ultimately complex productions that are built from that blueprint that not only add the visual and audible aspects, but involve dozens of other creative artists' input, from the director to the actors to the costume designers, set designers and more. It has been said that there are three movies: the movie that is written in the script, the movie that is shot and the movie that is edited. That is because each step of that process involves creative input and changes that shape the movie into its final form. That final form is sometimes a faithful adaptation of the original screenplay, and sometimes a very different creature altogether.

Many movies are adapted from books or other sources, but when it comes to "spec scripts" or scripts written on speculation by a writer (with the hope that he can sell it after it is written), it all begins with the script. As the mighty Steven Spielberg once said, "If it ain't on the page, it ain't on the stage." It is the script that launches the ship, it is the script that draws and even guides the producers, the director, the actors and many others. Like a blueprint for a building that draws contractors, carpenters, electricians and more to construct the final edifice.

A spec script is the first embodiment of the story that grabs the hearts and imaginations of its readers, that inspires them to get the resources together to make it into a movie. And the power of that blueprint is its ability to convey an entertaining story. In Hollywood, as in most of life, story is king.

But because a screenplay is a blueprint, it is a kind of unfinished "outline" for a movie. It does not convey many details like a novel can. For instance, a script gives brief descriptions of characters, and only passing references to locations where events take place. Casting, costuming, set design as well as music and other elements will all be added to the movie by other professionals who expand that original story into a multilayered existential work of art.

Apart from the use of some narration, a movie script does not delve much into the inner mental thoughts of characters. It is more external than a novel. More visual and active, because the final movie form will be visual and active. That is, the reader must infer what is going on inside the characters based on their behavior, choices and words.

Also, a screenplay must cover story ground in less time than other mediums like novels. For example, good dialogue is usually shorter, more economical, it communicates more in fewer words, driven in part by the fact that a movie is about one-and-a-half to two hours long which translates to roughly 120 pages in a script (1 page per minute of final screen time). And as you will see, those pages are not full of text like a book is. Everything is shorter, briefer, more concise, similar to how short stories are compared to novels.

In this sense, a screenplay reader must be more sophisticated and attentive in their reading. Every scene, every gesture, every visual reference, every word must have a purpose in a screenplay. And all of it ideally integrates into the meaning that the storyteller is conveying. Now, there are exceptions to all these things, but my main concern is to help prepare the reader of this series to read a bit differently than usual.

Because of this abbreviated "external" approach to storytelling, reading a script requires active engagement on the part of the reader, who must sometimes decipher meanings, symbols, and character motivations like a detective. But the effort is well worth it as the reader becomes more skilled at watching movies and television with greater appreciation.

So, the strength of a movie script is that it is the essence of the story, its heart and soul, the primal foundation upon which a movie is built and expanded. That is why I am publishing the Screenplays as Literature Series, because despite the format being an abbreviated starting point, it is still a powerful way to tell a great story, indeed, to visualize a movie before it is made.

Reading a screenplay can be like watching a movie in your mind.

Why This Series?

Most of the screenplays in the Screenplays as Literature Series are unproduced. That means they have not been sold or made into movies. One might therefore conclude that they are not very good stories if they could not garner the interest of producers to buy them.

I will let the reader be the final arbiter of that decision. But let me at least make the argument that it is also equally possible that there is plenty of other reasons why these screenplays could be very good stories and yet still not produced.

Everyone in Hollywood knows that there are too many excellent scripts that don't get made. Sometimes it's because they don't recognize truly unique genius (the secret desire of every writer). With the studio blockbuster mentality, many producers and studios are looking for "more of the same" to make big money fast: prequels, sequels, rip-offs and spin-offs. Many great movies, like Schindler's List and Forrest Gump had a history of being rejected by every major studio in town and taking as long as ten or more years to get made—by the biggest producers in town!

In Hollywood there are a million bad reasons why good scripts don't get sold or made. It could be political incorrectness or other "social justice" censorship, it could be budget, it could be scheduling conflicts, it could be sea changes at studios, it could be creative differences or infighting. Often, it's the worst reason in the world, and the most common: You don't know the right people at the right time.

It's actually a miracle that any movie gets made. So, a lot of good ones languish unread or unproduced on the shelves of writers and others who just couldn't get people to see their scripts were undiscovered Oscar winners. I say that, not sarcastically, but with full sincerity. I believe it. Although, I would have to walk back the "Oscar" praise, since the Academy Awards have increasingly become less a sign of recognized excellence and more a sign of inbred political incest.

There is something called "The Blacklist" every year that is a list of recent scripts in Hollywood that are considered excellent by many readers, that have made the rounds, that everyone "in the know" has read, that are excellent, but yet never get made for a multitude of these very reasons listed above.

So, the point is that "unproduced" does not necessarily mean "bad." Sadly, that means that both the genius and the self-deluded amateur are in the same boat. Neither of them knows if their rejected script is an undiscovered masterpiece or a rejected delusion of mediocrity.

Am I an undiscovered Mozart or am I simply Salieri?

Again, I will let you the reader decide when it comes to the scripts in this series.

I just hope you enjoy these stories as much as I enjoyed writing them.

Understanding the Format

I will describe how to understand some of the unique formatting of a screenplay to help avoid confusion for the reader not acquainted with script formatting.

My first and foremost advice is to try to picture yourself watching a movie as you read the text. This is, after all, a script for a movie. So why not read it that way? You will have to imagine a lot of details to fill in the gaps of what costume designers, make-up artists, set designers and others would normally bring to the production of the script. But some readers actually like doing that.

Maybe a character may remind you of your favorite actor. So, imagine that actor as you read their action and dialogue. But notice every detail, every nuance of dialogue, because, as I noted earlier, every single detail is there for a reason.

Though I have formatted these screenplays basically as they were written, I have made some changes to make it easier for readers who are not in the film business. Normally, screenplays are written in courier font. Courier is an ugly font, so in the print version of this script I changed it to a more legible one that most readers will be comfortable with. I want to make it easier for you, not harder.

If you are reading this in ebook format, you can alter the font and spacing, to whatever format you want to read it in.

But let's get going with our quick lesson on how to read a script.

Scene Headings

After reading, "FADE IN," the reader will first notice what is called a "Scene Heading." It looks something like this:

INT. DUNGEON CORRIDOR – NIGHT

This is the notation of the location where the next scene is taking place. It helps the moviemakers organize for their shooting, but for the reader, it tells us quickly where the scene takes place.

The first element will either be "**INT**." which stands for interior, or "**EXT**." which stands for exterior. So, we know if we are inside a location or outside.

The next element of the scene heading is the actual location, such as "**DUNGEON CORRIDOR**." It is the briefest way of referring to that location. If there is some description in the paragraph below it, it will be very sparse, like painting a quick emotional picture of the feel of where we are, as opposed to wordy detailed descriptions. So, you will have to conjure up in your own mind what it looks like, like the set designer and costume designer does later. Hey, you'll be like a movie director!

Then we have "**NIGHT**" or "**DAY**." These are also quick designations for the shooting schedule, but they also tell us as readers what part of a day we are in.

Sometimes, the scene headings are shortened. If you already established "EXT… DAY" and then follow the character walking into the house, you need to alert the reader that he is now in "INT," but you don't have to necessarily add "DAY" again, because it was a continuous movement. So be prepared for some shortened scene headings to make the reading flow smoother.

Action

Usually below that scene heading is what is called the "action." Here is what it looks like with a scene heading before it:

INT. DUNGEON CORRIDOR - NIGHT

TWO CLOAKED FIGURES slither through the shadows of a medieval dungeon corridor. SCREAMS of torture. Rats SQUEAL.

Action describes any actions of characters we will see. Again, it is sparse and to the point and focused on what we are going to see on the screen, not what is in the character's head. Every word counts.

And because of that economy of language, do not expect grammar that follows the Chicago Manual of Style. Sentence fragments often rule the day because they keep the pace moving, like you are watching a movie, rather than reading a novel.

Sometimes a writer may add a stylistic flourish and tell us what the reader should conclude based on what we are seeing. So, you might see something like, "He obviously doesn't want to go with her." This is internal and might only be conveyed in the facial gesture of the actor. But since we cannot see the actors in the script, writers must sometimes cheat to help the reader understand what the viewer of the movie will be more capable of seeing.

You will notice the ALL CAPS words. Usually, when a character shows up for the first time anywhere in the script, their names are in all caps. It is a way of easily finding them for the movie makers, but it also helps the reader realize a new presence in the story.

Also, as in the example above, special effects, such as sounds or visual effects, are also capitalized to bring notice to the filmmakers for their production purposes. For the reader, this alerts us to the importance of a sound or image that would be more obvious to a movie viewer than a script reader.

This goes for underlined words as well. Underlining is like focusing the camera on something.

Sometimes, the scene headings and action can be used in a simpler format to differentiate complex action or visuals within a single location. You want it to read easily and quickly so you get a sense of the pace of the scene and aren't slowed down by details. Here is an example:

SLOW MOTION SHOT

Dragut's warhorse breaks through the cloud of smoke and fighting. He sees La Valette against a flagpole.

STARKEY AND THE MONSTER

Back up against the wall. A whack by the Monster snaps one of Starkey's swords in two.

LA VALETTE AND DRAGUT

battle around the flagpole. With a CLANG, their blades cross against the pole and freeze, straining against each other.

In this example, we are in one location, and two fights are going on that would be easily edited visually to follow for the audience. But for the reader, I tell them that first, they see a SLOW MOTION SHOT of the bad guy Dragut arriving. Then we jump over to a battle between the two characters STARKEY AND THE MONSTER, and then a jump back to Dragut who is now fighting the character LaValette.

Sometimes you might see something like this:

SUPER: ISTANBUL, TURKEY

This is called a "super" and it is short for "superimposed." It's basically like those titles we see at the bottom of the screen when we are introduced to a new location or to some introductory material like that famous screen-crawl at the beginning of each Star Wars movie.

Dialogue

When characters speak in a script, this is what it looks like:

GUARD
Ho. Where does ye think yer goin'?
(beat)
Ya looks shady to me.

The character's name is in all caps, so we clearly know who is speaking from what is being said. Before a character speaks, they must be described as present in the action first. Otherwise, they are popping in like a quantum fluctuation, which would be confusing to us Newtonian readers :-).

But also notice the word "beat" in parentheses. These are called, quite helpfully, "parentheticals," and they are used for several purposes. The word "beat" above, simply means a meaningful pause. It will affect the context of the words spoken or indicates a change of direction in dialogue. You can imagine the character pausing before they say their next lines, which adds nuance to the dialogue.

You might also read parentheticals with descriptions like "sarcastic," or "angrily," or something similar.

JANE
(sarcastic)
Don't you look pretty.

This is done when the words themselves may not obviously communicate to the reader what a viewer can see on the screen. "Don't you look pretty" could be either genuine or sarcastic and you might not be able to determine that unless you saw the actress saying it with her facial gestures. So, the writer cheats a bit to help us catch what we cannot see.

You might also read an action in the parenthetical like "(To the other guy)" or "(he looks closer)." These would be used to describe actions done in the middle of talking, such as changing the character to whom they are talking.

Sometimes, you might see the unique parentheticals, (O.S.) and (V.O.) after the character name rather than below it:

JOHN (O.S.)
Put that gun down.

JANE (V.O.)
I realized John was not everything he said he was.

(O.S.) means "off-screen." It means that we hear the voice of the character, but we do not see them as we are watching the "movie in our minds." They are outside the camera view, but still in the scene.

(V.O.) means "voice-over," and is used when the character's voice is a narrator that is not within the actual story but is commenting upon it from outside the story. It's narration.

Well, there it is, your quick lesson on script-reading. It's not much different than reading plays. If you know the basic elements, it becomes quite easy to watch the movie in your mind as you read the script!

Introduction to Nietzsche: A Dangerous Life Screenplay

I first wrote this Nietzsche script in 1997, and over the years, did rewrites, including some help on the story from fellow Nietzsche-appreciator, Adam Christing. It was originally called *Friedrich and Elisabeth*, because it is ostensibly a story about brother and sister. But in the end, the name Nietzsche is just way too famous and way too cool for a title, so I changed it to the current one.

Here's the pitch:

Nietzsche: A Dangerous Life

His ideas would change the world.

Her obsession would drive him mad.

A bond between brother and sister

only God could separate.

The true story of Friedrich Nietzsche, the scandalous atheist philosopher who went insane, and Elisabeth, his beloved religious sister who tried to stop him.

Nietzsche: A Dangerous Life is a story of passion, propriety and taboo, and the fight of one man's reason against the ticking clock of his own insanity.

I researched Friedrich Nietzsche very heavily, reading from all of his works and a dozen biographies. He is one of the most well-known, and yet least understood, philosophers of history. Part of the problem is that he wrote contradictory statements in different works, and in others he was opaque and poetic rather than rationally explaining clear and distinct ideas. This was deliberate of course, as he disdained modernity and its Cartesian trappings.

Because of this, there are many differing theories of what he was actually saying. Some consider him a nihilist, who rejected all forms of modern knowledge and truth. Others say he was anti-nihilist, who criticized relativism. So, the man was an enigma, which makes for a fascinating character to explore.

He was also an infamous atheist in Europe, in an era when it was not socially acceptable to be one. Because Friedrich was raised in a strong Lutheran Victorian culture, he adopted those social morals and manners even though he wrote against them. He behaved in a quite proper and socially acceptable way, unlike other atheists in history, known for their libertinism, like Lou von Salomé or Bertrand Russell. And Friedrich suffered because of it. He lived sentimentally as a Christian, while trying to undermine Christianity. He desired a traditional romantic love relationship with the very libertine women whose promiscuity and autonomy his ideas empowered.

Thus, one of the themes in this script is about living contradictions, how we say one thing but often fail to live consistently, how we do not desire the consequences of our own ideas: the frailty of human nature, all too human. You will find in this story that Friedrich is not the only one with this problem. Almost all the characters, including the protagonist, Franz Overbeck, seem to wrestle with this cognitive dissonance in one way or another. It reveals an aspect of human nature as being self-deceived, self-justifying, and quite incapable of being the masters of our fate and captains of our souls that we think we are.

Speaking of Franz Overbeck, I chose to make him the protagonist of the story. He was Nietzsche's best friend for many years, and he was an interesting ally, whose biography contained the most fascinating interpretation of Nietzsche's mental illness. By now, the reader is most likely aware that Friedrich Nietzsche went mad in his later years. Like everything else about this enigmatic larger than life little guy, there are different theories as to why. I tried to include all possibilities within this story to give every view its due. But Overbeck's is the most thought-provoking in its ramifications. I won't spoil it for you by explaining it here.

Another theme I address in the script is about religion and faith versus skepticism and doubt in this modern world. In a sense, Nietzsche was the harbinger of the post-modern world. His ideas undergird much of contemporary thought in western culture, from nihilism and moral relativism to Christophobic hatred. He is a turning point of history, and that's what makes his story so important. But here's the thing: everyone assumes Christianity is about religion and faith, and science is about knowledge and skepticism. But is this really true? Nietzsche rejected Christianity, but he knew that something would have to take its place. And that something would operate very much like a religion. So, can we ever really escape that "God-shaped vacuum" in our hearts that Blaise Pascal wrote of?

A powerful expression of this tension between religion and atheism was embodied in Friedrich's relationship with his sister Elisabeth. This is why the screenplay is a kind of "love story" between brother and sister. Not an incestuous romance, but a familial love and worship that incarnates the struggle between the ancient and the modern, between faith and doubt, Christianity and atheism. Both Friedrich and Elisabeth were raised as Lutheran believers, but while Friedrich abandoned his faith, Elisabeth did not. She remained religiously devout and yet also remained devout in her love for her brother to the very end, creating a "love/hate" relationship with its own contradictions.

And Elisabeth's religious devotion is not without nuance or tragedy itself, as Elisabeth also followed the path of anti-Semitism that plagued Germany's culture.

Her faith became corrupted. Ah, the contradictions of human nature abound. Do they point to the need for something transcendent, or do they merely encapsulate the tragic nihilism of imminence?

Those familiar with Nietzsche's works will recognize that quite a bit of Friedrich's dialogue in the script is drawn from his written words (I've done this with Ritschl, Wagner and others in the script as well). I wanted to give context to his famous philosophical statements, to show how they might have grown organically from his experience, as well as expressing his dramatic spirit truthfully. Drama is a powerful way of showing abstract concepts lived out concretely in a life.

And most of the historical characters in the script, like Wagner, Cosima, Ritschl, Rée, Förster, Lou von Salomé and others are based on research as well. I tried to capture Nietzsche's relationships with accuracy, despite some creative license. That includes his infamous relationship with the composer Wagner as well. Many of the significant incidents in this script really happened, which is what makes it so captivating. I would argue that reading this script gives the reader more than an entertaining story about an historical character; It gives an accurate picture of the heart and soul of this tragic anti-hero's life.

That's what this story is: a tragedy, like the movie, *Amadeus*. But it is also a kind of detective story, an archeological exploration of origins to help us understand that ideas have consequences.

Brian James Godawa
Author and Screenwriter, Nietzsche: A Dangerous Life

"NIETZSCHE: A DANGEROUS LIFE"

PITCH BLACK SCREEN

A strong, wise ELDERLY MAN'S VOICE narrates from the blackness. A voice of nobility and grace, yet sober with experience. There is nothing new under the sun to this storyteller.

> NARRATOR (V.O.)
> Once upon a time there lived a madman who ran
> to the marketplace and cried, "I seek God!"
> "Where is God," he cried. "I shall tell you. We
> have killed him -- you and I. All of us are his
> murderers."

A child's SCREAM pierces the darkness.

INT. TRAIN - DAY

The scream belongs to a SMALL BOY running up the aisle of a rickety 1800s train. He jumps into his MOTHER'S arms.

Across from her is FRANZ OVERBECK, 63. A dignified man, calm and rational. Well-groomed, but not vain. He returns to reading his book.

> NARRATOR (V.O.)
> "How shall we, the murderers of all murderers,
> comfort ourselves? Who will wipe his blood off
> us?"

The train stops. Overbeck closes the book: "THUS SPOKE ZARATHUSTRA" BY FRIEDRICH NIETZSCHE.

EXT. WEIMAR TRAIN STATION - DAY

> SUPER: WEIMAR, GERMANY - 1899.

The whistle BLOWS, Steam HISSES. Overbeck jumps off with his overstuffed attaché case. He makes his way through the bustling crowd.

> NARRATOR (V.O.)
> Here the madman fell silent. Then he said, "I come
> too early." My time has not yet come.

EXT. VILLA SILBERBLICK, WEIMAR - DAY

A modest two-story villa overlooks Weimar from the foothills.

> WOMAN'S V.O.
> Ssshhhhh!

INT. VILLA SILBERBLICK STAIRWELL - DAY

ELISABETH NIETZSCHE, 54, holds back a small crowd of visiting CURIOSITY SEEKERS at the doorway to an upstairs room. She is a pleasant Victorian socialite who looks younger than her years and more upper-society than she acts.

A woman GIGGLES. The curiosity seekers look at one another nervously. One of them whispers.

> FEMALE VISITOR
> Will he attack us?

Another anonymous GIGGLE.

> ELISABETH
> No. He's very complacent. Just remember, this is
> my brother, not a circus animal.

Elisabeth holds the door with dramatic pause.

> ELISABETH
> Ladies and gentlemen, I present to you, Friedrich
> Nietzsche, the mad philosopher!

Elisabeth opens the door wide and walks into the room.

INT. FRIEDRICH'S UPSTAIRS ROOM

Through the doorway, the visitors can see him in his bed at the far corner of the room:

FRIEDRICH NIETZSCHE. He sits upright in his bed. His white gown and bedsheets give him the look of a holy man. His signature big burly mustache covers his mouth like a bush. His hair matted and unkempt. He stares into the void, utterly unaware of the circus animal he has indeed become.

The visitors hold back. Elisabeth waves them in.

>ELISABETH
>
>Just be quiet.

The crowd cautiously enters the sparsely arranged room and stays at a safe distance.

>FEMALE VISITOR (O.S.)
>
>Poor man.

>MALE VISITOR (O.S.)
>
>Ssshh!

Elisabeth bends down and whispers lovingly to Friedrich. Her commitment and dedication to him is deep.

>ELISABETH
>
>Hello, dear Fritz. It's your little Llama.

Friedrich looks up at her. A SIGH of surprise from someone.

But he glazes over. Doesn't recognize his sister. Turns back to his eternal recurring stare into oblivion.

Elisabeth's smile cannot hide her pain.

>MALE VISITOR (O.S.)
>
>It's a bit of a letdown, I must say.

Elisabeth looks at the crowd, regretting she let them in.

EXT. VILLA SILBERBLICK - DAY

Overbeck walks up to the front door of the villa. The door has a big golden "N" posted on it. It's ajar. He walks in.

INT. VILLA SILBERBLICK DOWNSTAIRS LIVING ROOM

Overbeck looks around. Signs of a party. A table of food, glasses of wine. He hears a SOUND upstairs.

INT. FRIEDRICH'S UPSTAIRS ROOM

The crowd is still staring at the "mad philosopher."

The door crashes open. A shudder through the crowd. Overbeck enters with the wrath of God on his face.

ELISABETH
Franz! Ladies and gentlemen, Professor Franz
Overbeck. A close friend of Friedrich's from Basel.

OVERBECK
Elisabeth, may I have a word with you, alone?

ELISABETH
(to the crowd)
Will you excuse us?

The crowd uncomfortably files past the steaming Overbeck.

The door closes. Overbeck and Elisabeth whisper, trying not to be heard by
Friedrich.

OVERBECK
What in hell are you doing?

ELISABETH
What do you mean?

OVERBECK
You know what I mean. Have you no respect for
his dignity?

ELISABETH
I beg your pardon.

OVERBECK
Parading him around like -- like some kind of --
freak?

ELISABETH
He is not a freak!
      (catches herself)
Franz, when my brother was sane, no one would
listen to him. And that was all he wanted, was to
be listened to. Now the world is crowing at his
feet. And why? Because I have had the courage to
offer him to the world, madness and all.

FRIEDRICH (O.S.)
I am Dionysus! I am Christ!

They pull away out of Friedrich's earshot.

OVERBECK
And what is in this for you, Elisabeth?

ELISABETH
Why do you accuse me, so? I have dedicated my
life to my brother and the publication of his
philosophy.

OVERBECK
You don't even believe in his philosophy.

ELISABETH
That's not true. People misunderstand him and
what he was trying to say.

Overbeck turns to the bookshelf and scans it, looking for something. He finds it.
A manuscript. He pulls it out.

OVERBECK
Then why don't you publish this?

It is: "ANTICHRIST" BY FRIEDRICH NIETZSCHE.

She grabs the book from him and puts it back on the shelf where it belongs.

ELISABETH
The Prussian blasphemy laws make anti-religious
literature illegal. Would you prefer to see the poor
invalid in jail?

OVERBECK
Friedrich would.

An outburst of LAUGHTER erupts from downstairs. Friedrich MIMICS THE
LAUGHTER mindlessly.

ELISABETH
I really must get back to my party.

(she turns to leave)
Oh, did you remember to bring your
correspondence with Fritz?

OVERBECK
No. I -- I'll bring the letters next trip.

ELISABETH
I'm writing a biography of Fritz's life. I think
you'll be impressed with the image I create of him.

Overbeck does not respond. Elisabeth leaves. He looks over at Friedrich with
pathos.

OVERBECK
Creating him in your own image.

He sits on a chair next to the bed. Opens his attaché case. Pulls out a pile of
papers: Friedrich's letters to Overbeck. He lied to Elisabeth.

He puts the papers back in the case. Overbeck looks upon his oblivious friend
with a heavy heart.

NARRATOR (V.O.)
"O what a noble mind is here o'erthrown! O, how
life has become but a tale told by an idiot, full of
sound and fury, signifying..."

As if finishing the Narrator's line, Friedrich blurts out.

FRIEDRICH
...NOTHING!

Overbeck looks at his frail friend with sad empathy.

NARRATOR (V.O.)
What brought on this curse of madness? This body
of frailty? Why did the madman go insane? It has
been said that the end of a thing can be found in
its beginning. So that is where our tale must go.
Back to the beginning...

FRIEDRICH
(whimpering scared)
No. No. No.

EXT. GERMAN COUNTRYSIDE - DAY

SUPER: 1849

Vast, fertile, wide open expanse at the foot of the rolling hills near Thuringia, Germany. God's country.

NARRATOR (V.O.)
He was born in a small town in lower Germany, to
a pious Lutheran father whom he adored. It was a
storybook life.

In a small pond surrounded by willow trees on the edge of eternity stand a father and son fishing.

The father, KARL NIETZSCHE, 36, helps his son, young FIVE-YEAR OLD FRIEDRICH, to prepare his pole. Friedrich is all smiles.

Karl looks up happily into the sky, closes his eyes in thankfulness. Friedrich imitates his hero.

EXT. NIETZSCHE PARSONAGE, GARDEN - DAY

Friedrich now helps his Father plant some bulbs in their family garden behind their home.

Karl does the work while Friedrich eagerly watches.

KARL
Friedrich. Do not be deceived: God is not mocked.
A man reaps what he sows.
(pulls out a diseased bulb)
If you sow sin, you will reap destruction.
(pulls out a healthy bulb)
If you sow grace, you will reap eternal life.

Friedrich listens with devotion, though he doesn't really understand.

FRIEDRICH
Yes, papa!

Karl stops and grabs his temple in migraine pain.

> FRIEDRICH
> What's wrong, papa?

> KARL
> (shakes it off)
> Nothing. Just a headache. Now, go get ready for
> church.

> FRIEDRICH
> Yes, papa!

INT. LUTHERAN CHURCH - DAY

Karl preaches in the pulpit of the church dressed in minister's robes. He is the pastor.

His family sits proudly in the front pews: FRANZISKA, his 26-year old devoted Victorian wife; 3-YEAR OLD ELISABETH; and Friedrich, eyes fixed on his father, mouth open in rapt attention.

> KARL
> Then Job responded, "The hand of the Lord has
> done this, in whose hand is the life of every living
> thing. He captures the wise in their own deceit. He
> inflicts pain and gives relief. He deprives the
> leaders of the earth of their reason and makes
> them wander in a pathless waste. Shall we indeed
> accept good from God and not accept adversity?
> The Lord gave and the Lord has taken away.
> Blessed be the name of the Lord."

EXT. RÖCKEN HILL - DAY

Little Friedrich stands reading his Bible as his father's preaching continues as VOICE-OVER. An EAGLE'S CRY catches his attention.

He looks up with awe at the huge Gothic cathedral before him. The wind stirs like a spirit through the picturesque outdoors all around him.

Precocious little Elisabeth watches a horse tied up by the post. It NEIGHS uneasily. She runs scared over to Friedrich.

> ELISABETH
>
> Fritz!

He remains obliviously reading his Bible.

> ELISABETH
>
> Fritz! Herr Müller says you shouldn't be reading
> at such a young age.

> FRIEDRICH
>
> That's because I'm a prodigy, silly goose. And I
> want to be like papa someday. A minister of God.

She doesn't follow.

> ELISABETH
>
> Come play with me, Fritz.

He pulls her over to look down upon the small town of Röcken nestled in the foothills.

> FRIEDRICH
>
> Look at that, Elisabeth. It feels like God looking
> down upon the world.
>   (beat)
> I think God has something important planned for
> me.

> ELISABETH
>
> That's why papa says you're his Little Minister!

Elisabeth reaches up and grabs his cap and runs for it.

> FRIEDRICH
>
> Why you! I'm going to eat you!

He chases his giggling sister, making sure he holds back so as not to catch her too easily.

> ELISABETH
>
> Little Minister! Little Minister!

EXT. CHURCH GRAVEYARD

They run into the church graveyard and end up by their picnic basket and blanket. Friedrich catches her, tickling her.

> ELISABETH
> Stop it! Stop it!

She loves it. He stops.

> ELISABETH
> What did you stop for?

> FRIEDRICH
> You told me to.

> ELISABETH
> No, I didn't.

> FRIEDRICH
> Oh, yes you did.

He tickles her again. She laughs like a little princess. Finally, he stops and they rest.

> FRIEDRICH
> Let's make an oath.

> ELISABETH
> What's an oath?

> FRIEDRICH
> It's an eternal promise.

> ELISABETH
> I like that!

> FRIEDRICH
> Okay, raise your right hand.

He models, she follows.

> FRIEDRICH
> I, Elisabeth Nietzsche...

ELISABETH
That's my name, silly.

FRIEDRICH
I know. You're supposed to say after me. I,
Elisabeth...

ELISABETH
I, Elisabeth...

FRIEDRICH
Do solemnly swear...

ELISABETH
Do solemnly swear... What does that mean?

FRIEDRICH
It means, you solemnly swear.

ELISABETH
Oh.

FRIEDRICH
That I will live forever and only...

ELISABETH
I will live forever and only...

FRIEDRICH
(meaning it himself)
For God and Jesus...

ELISABETH
For God and Jesus...

FRIEDRICH
And for my darling sweet brother, Friedrich.

ELISABETH
And for my darling sourpuss brother, Friedrich.

FRIEDRICH
You!

He tickles her again.

ELISABETH

Now you promise.

FRIEDRICH

If you can catch me, I will.

He pops up and they run out of the graveyard.

EXT. CHURCH HILL - DAY

At the crest of the hill, he stops and lets her catch up. He leads her down the hill.

FRIEDRICH

I'm going to call you my faithful little Llama.

Elisabeth smiles broadly. Then turns puzzled.

ELISABETH

What's a Llama?

FRIEDRICH

It's an animal that's loyal to the death.

ELISABETH

I'm your little Llama!

FRIEDRICH

And when it doesn't like you, it spits at you.

He fake spits at her and runs off. She follows.

INT. NIETZSCHE PARSONAGE, LIVING ROOM - NIGHT

Their middle class quaint little home. Friedrich kneels in prayer beside the small bed of sleeping sister Elisabeth. A loyal mutt of a dog lays next to him.

FRIEDRICH

And thank you for mother, and for sister
Elisabeth...

He peeks open his eye to look at his sister sleeping in her bed. He smiles and continues.

FRIEDRICH

...And most of all, for papa. Make me just like my
papa, dear Jesus.

He pulls out a little crucifix and softly slips it into Elisabeth's curled hands.

He hears a SOUND outside. In an instant, he pops up and runs through the house.

> FRIEDRICH
> Papa is home!

INT. NIETZSCHE KITCHEN

He runs up to the door. Mother Franziska works her way to the wood burning stove with pots boiling.

> FRANZISKA
> Now be kind to your father.

> FRIEDRICH
> Yes, Mamma!

> FRANZISKA
> Talk softly.

> FRIEDRICH
> Yes, Mamma!

> FRANZISKA
> Remember his headaches!

> FRIEDRICH
> Yes, Mamma!

He opens the door. Down in the stairwell pastor Karl stands holding his head in pain again. He looks up and smiles at Friedrich, trying to hide his migraine.

> FRIEDRICH
> Papa!

> KARL
> Hello, Friedrich. How's my Little Minister?

INT. LIVING ROOM

The mutt is propped up against the window and sees a DARK HORSE tied up outside. It looks up at the window.

The dog jumps down and runs toward the kitchen, BARKING.

INT. KITCHEN STAIRWAY

Karl starts up the stairs. Stumbles a bit in pain. Friedrich doesn't understand.

The Mutt runs down the stairs, throwing Karl off balance.

> FRIEDRICH
>
> Papa!!

Karl loses balance and falls backward.

> FRIEDRICH
>
> Pappaaaaaa!!!!

INT. LITTLE FRIEDRICH'S BEDROOM - DAY

Little Friedrich stands before a mirror, all spiffed up with hair oiled back, and bawling his eyes out.

Franziska tightens his tie and shirt buttons. She's dressed in black with shawl.

> FRANZISKA
>
> Now, Friedrich, you must be strong.

Franziska turns him to see THREE WOMEN standing in a row.

> FRANZISKA
>
> We won't be alone. We're going to have some
> family stay with us for a while.

Friedrich calms as Franziska introduces each one.

> FRANZISKA
>
> Grandmama.

GRANDMA NIETZSCHE, also in black, smiles toothlessly through what has to be hundreds of years of wrinkles, clutching her 1000-year old Bible.

> FRANZISKA
>
> Aunt Rosalie.

AUNT ROSALIE, 200 pounds of smothering German motherliness.

> AUNT ROSALIE
>
> Fear not, little one. No purpose of God's can be
> thwarted.

FRANZISKA
And Auntie Augusta.

AUNTIE AUGUSTA, The sweetest little woman in all of Germany, with the ugliest face in all the world.

AUNT AUGUSTA
The Lord is my shepherd, I shall not want.

Friedrich pulls back and breaks out crying again.

INT. LUTHERAN CATHEDRAL - DAY

Lutheran funeral: A casket up front, a PASTOR in the pulpit.

PASTOR
Dearly beloved. Blessed are those who die in the
Lord. For who shall separate us from the love of
Christ?

As the Pastor eulogizes, little Friedrich and Elisabeth sit in the pew, smashed in between Mother, Grandma, Aunts Rosalie and Augusta. All the women are bawling their eyes out.

But Friedrich is icy, his gaze fixed with utter hatred upon the huge crucifix at the front of the sanctuary.

The pastor's words fade completely out of Friedrich's hearing.

NARRATOR (V.O.)
When the heart is hardened, love becomes hatred.
Faith turns to doubt. A funeral for a father
becomes a funeral for God.

INT. LUTHERAN CATHEDRAL - LATER

The mourners finish leaving the church with the casket. Little Friedrich stands up front in the sanctuary.

He turns to look back up at the crucifix with still angry eyes, now red with tears. The hatred seethes up in him and he whispers.

FRIEDRICH
You killed him. You killed papa.

(beat)
I'll never forgive you. Never.

INT. TRAVELLING TRAIN - DAY

BACK TO THE PRESENT. 63-year old Overbeck sits in his train car traveling home. He has been reading Friedrich's letters.

Overbeck takes out the manuscript he rescued from Elisabeth, THE ANTICHRIST. Checks more letters.

                    NARRATOR (V.O.)
          Ressentiment is the dread feeling of impotence in
          the face of one's enemy. Followed by the instinct
          of revenge as a means of endurance.
                    (beat)
          Belief in God is not the projection of man's wish
          fulfillment. The rejection of God is.

EXT. NIETZSCHE NAUMBURG HOME - DAY

                    SUPER: Naumburg, Germany - 1864

EXT. NAUMBURG HILL - DAY

Another beautiful surrounding of mountainous outdoor Germany. Friedrich, NOW 20 YEARS OLD, sits morosely staring up at the mountains.

Elisabeth, NOW 18, picks flowers. Friedrich walks down the hill trance-like. Elisabeth runs after him.

                    ELISABETH
          Fritz! Fritz!!

She catches up to him at the bottom of the hill.

EXT. NAUMBURG TOWN STREET

They walk through the town. She chatters on.

                    ELISABETH
          Oh, Fritz, I'm going to miss you dreadfully. Don't
          forget to take your headache medicine and wear

your glasses when you read, and don't let the girls
take your mind off your studies.

> FRIEDRICH
> Yes, mother.

He smirks playfully. She kisses him on the cheek.

> FRANZISKA (O.S.)
> Friedrich! Friedrich, your carriage is ready to
> leave! Hurry up!

Franziska, Rosalie and Augusta wave kerchiefs from the door of their home.
Friedrich grabs Elisabeth's hand and runs to the carriage.

EXT. NIETZSCHE NAUMBURG HOME

As Friedrich and Elisabeth reach the carriage, the three little ladies, also a bit
older, greet him like a row of clucking hens. First, he hugs Rosalie.

> AUNT ROSALIE
> Don't let your learning hamper your spiritual
> duties.

> FRIEDRICH
> We'll see about that, Aunt Rosalie.

He smiles teasingly. She smiles. He moves on to hug Augusta.

> FRIEDRICH
> Aunt Augusta.

> AUNT AUGUSTA
> He who believes in the Son has eternal life...

She waits for him to finish. He does so reluctantly.

> FRIEDRICH
> But he who does not obey the Son shall not see
> life....

> FRIEDRICH AND AUNT AUGUSTA
> But the wrath of God abides on him.

Augusta smiles proudly, entirely ignorant of Friedrich's condescension. He
moves on to Franziska.

FRIEDRICH

Mother.

FRANZISKA

Your papa would be so proud of you.

He embraces her, a look of bitter pain on his face.

Elisabeth sneaks up next to Franziska to be last in line.

The horses act restless.

HORSEMAN

Let's go, boy!

Elisabeth opens her arms wide for a hug. Friedrich obliges.

ELISABETH

I wish I could come with you.

FRIEDRICH

Silly goose. You have your own education to
worry about.

Elisabeth reaches behind her neck and pulls off a necklace and hands it to
Friedrich. It's a crucifix.

ELISABETH

I want you to have this.

Friedrich is touched, but reluctantly so. All four women are BAWLING.
Elisabeth holds Franziska. Friedrich smiles.

FRIEDRICH

You should see yourselves.

The women all stop for a moment and look at each other. Then they break out in
CRYING LAUGHTER.

Friedrich jumps up into the carriage. The women wave their kerchiefs. He waves
back and the Horseman carries him away. The women abruptly return to their
crying.

NARRATOR (V.O.)

His beloved family did not realize they were
saying goodbye forever...

INT. HORSE CARRIAGE

Friedrich sighs. Stares angrily at Elisabeth's crucifix. Clasps it into a tight fist of vexation. It pierces his skin drawing blood.

> NARRATOR (V.O.)
> He was finally free. Free to pursue his heart's
> desire. Fulfill his vow to God...

EXT. UNIVERSITY OF BONN, GERMANY - NIGHT

EST. SHOT of the campus. Dark, dead trees hang over the walkways. Bookish students and pedantic professors tread the icy snow, undaunted by the harsh German winter.

INT. BONN CLASSROOM - DAY

Young Friedrich sits in a lecture hall, well-dressed, but wrapped in heavy clothes and scarf. His breath, visible.

In walks PROFESSOR RITSCHL, hard-nosed, but passionate about one thing, and one thing only: Philology, the study of language. He's a force of energy underneath a pale, skeletal exterior. The students hush. Ritschl looks around at them like a king with his vassals.

Students shiver, rub their hands and blow into them. Friedrich puts on his circular reading glasses. Stares intensely with paper and pencil ready.

Ritschl speaks while looking exclusively at Friedrich.

> RITSCHL
> "Nature shows that with the growth of
> intelligence comes increased capacity for pain, and
> it is only with the highest degree of intelligence
> that suffering reaches its supreme point."
> Schopenhauer.

Friedrich writes it down.

Ritschl pauses. Looks around again. Nothing but gaping mouths and boggled minds. He continues.

RITSCHL

Most of you will leave this university and utterly
fail and die because you will not have the will to
live. The will to survive.

Students glance nervously at each other with confusion. Friedrich smiles slyly.

RITSCHL

The rest of you, a mere handful, are why I am
here. It is my intent to destroy everything you've
ever been taught. Your religion, your tradition,
your "culture." And give you a new religion -- of
reason. You will be the gods of the future. You
will stand alone and fully free from the shackles of
society and society's God.

Ritschl is looking straight at Friedrich, who returns the gaze with equal intensity.
This is exactly what Friedrich is looking for.

INT. FRIEDRICH'S DORM ROOM - NIGHT

Friedrich studies with a pile of books on his desk. He stops. Pulls his reading
glasses off. Rubs his eyes with strain. Migraine headache. But go on he must.
And another thing to notice is how sharply Friedrich dresses, even when
studying.

A KNOCK at his door jolts him. Groggily, he gets up and answers it. FIVE
FRATERNITY MEMBERS plow into his room.

The lead guy, FRENCHIE, a tall scrawny French boy, steps out from the group.
He's a bit hesitant, respectful to Friedrich.

FRENCHIE

Friedrich?

He looks guiltily at the others. Friedrich is impatient. Frenchie pulls out a Bible.

FRENCHIE

Well, we were just wondering. If we confess our
sins, God forgives us, right?

>   FRIEDRICH
>   (sarcastic)
>   So, the "Good Book" says.

>   FRENCHIE
>   Well, then. Do you think God would mind if we
>   just go out and sin a little, just so long as we
>   confess it afterwards?

Friedrich stares at him incredulously. The others shift about nervously.

>   FRIEDRICH
>   Well, my fellow positivists, there's only one way
>   to find out, now, isn't there?
>   (mischievous grin)
>   Scientific experimentation.

INT. BONN BORDELLO - NIGHT

Friedrich busts open the doors to the bordello, walking boldly in, followed by his five nervous frat boys. They look scared at the ladies of the night staring back at them.

Friedrich looks over the women with confidence.

>   FRIEDRICH
>   And some say there is no God.

INT. BONN BORDELLO - LATER

The five fraternity fellows hang around the living room. A Christmas tree in the corner, complete with manger, Blessed Virgin and Child. They're laughing, drinking and smooching with the whores, who condescend to the young fools.

Friedrich sits in a love seat, eagerly awaiting his pleasure. A girl steps up to him. Opens her robe.

His eyes brighten with lust. At his level, he sees only her body. And what a body. Buxom curves bursting the seams of silken veil.

And then she sits down. Her face is ugly as sin. God's sick sense of humor.

>   UGLY GIRL
>   My name's Hildegard.

Friedrich tightens. Eyes go wide in horror. Frenchie walks up to him with a tramp in his arms.

> FRENCHIE
> Hey, Nietzsche! Better discharge some of that
> semen of yours before it backs up into your brain
> and makes you go insane!

Frenchie WHINNIES and stomps like a stallion. Others laugh.

> FRAT BOY
> A horse! My kingdom for a horse!

More LAUGHS. Frenchie goes upstairs with his tramp. Friedrich spies a piano. He pops up and runs over to it.

The ugly one follows him and stands behind him as he plays a composition.

Another frat guy with strumpet in arm walks up the stairs. Then two more. Two left.

Friedrich grabs an unfinished shot of whiskey on the piano. Downs it, grimaces, and plays on. Three whores walk up to the piano in excitement.

> WHORE 1
> Can you play Wagner?

> WHORE 2
> Yes, Wagner! We love Wagner!

> WHORE 3
> He's so romantic!

Friedrich pauses, then bursts into "The Bridal March" from Wagner's Lohengrin. The last two guys go up the stairs.

The remaining five women gather around Friedrich. The ugly girl breaks out into an incredible solo. Libertine libretto. Obviously missed her calling.

INT. DOCTOR'S OFFICE - DAY

Friedrich sits on the exam table. A big burly DOCTOR with a Bismarck beard, one arm and a wandering eye, examines Friedrich's lymph nodes. He's suspicious of Friedrich. He goes over it one more time.

DR. BISMARCK

When did the lesions appear?

FRIEDRICH

Two weeks ago.

DR. BISMARCK

But you've had fevers and headaches for years.

FRIEDRICH

And stomach problems.

DR. BISMARCK

But it doesn't hurt when you urinate.

FRIEDRICH

No.

Dr. Bismarck stares at him with distrust. Friedrich fidgets.

DR. BISMARCK

Friedrich, if I didn't know you better, I'd say you have syphilis.

Friedrich looks at him with shock.

DR. BISMARCK

But your symptoms are incomplete and your history of problems too long. You need to slow down. You're studying too hard.

FRIEDRICH

I can't sleep.

Dr. Bismarck hands him a bottle and dropper.

DR. BISMARCK

I'll give you these Sydenham drops. Don't overdo the prescription. It's an opiate. God knows I don't want another addict.

FRIEDRICH

Don't worry. I prefer pain.

Dr. Bismarck eyes him with concern. Friedrich takes the bottle.

EXT. NAUMBURG STREETS - DAY

ESTABLISHING SHOT of the city streets lined with well-wishers. Shop fronts are decorated for Easter.

> NARRATOR (V.O.)
> "I am a wanderer," he said to himself. Free-spirit
> without a home. The homeless man.

INT. DINING AREA NIETZSCHE HOME, NAUMBURG - DAY

The dining table is set for an ornate Easter dinner. Franziska is moving back and forth placing final touches. Aunt Rosalie helps. They bump into each other and laugh.

INT. HALLWAY NIETZSCHE HOME

Elisabeth touches up a flower arrangement before a mirror. She's dressed in Victorian best. She picks at her hair for perfection. But she stops at the sound of a LOUD HORSE WHINNY outside. She grins and breathes a deep sigh.

The door opens and Elisabeth turns. It's Friedrich.

> ELISABETH
> Fritz!

He looks up at Elisabeth. Smiles broadly. Opens his arms. She floats down the stairs and jumps into his arms. He swings her around. He has the beginning of what will grow into his signature mustache.

Franziska and Rosalie arrive and the four of them hug. Friedrich kisses Franziska.

Elisabeth's eyes spark jealousy and she grabs Friedrich and kisses him away from mother.

> FRIEDRICH
> It's been too long.

Elisabeth turns a tad scolding.

> ELISABETH
> Weeks turned into months.

> FRIEDRICH
> My studies.

He COUGHS. Franziska and Elisabeth look worried at him.

> AUNT ROSALIE
> You must be famished! Let's eat!

Everyone looks at Rosalie. They know who's the hungry one around here. And they all laugh as she turns beet red.

INT. KITCHEN TABLE - LATER

Friedrich, Franziska, Elisabeth and Rosalie eat their Easter meal of ham and trimmings. Elisabeth offers Friedrich a bowl of dressing. He declines.

> ELISABETH
> It's Easter, Friedrich. Celebrate a little.

> AUNT ROSALIE
> Our Lord has risen.

> FRIEDRICH
> Too spicy. My stomach hasn't gotten any better.

> ELISABETH
> I should examine you myself.

> FRIEDRICH
> Tell us of the University at Leipzig, Elisabeth.

> ELISABETH
> (to the women)
> Well... I'll never be as brilliant as Fritz.
>
> (to Friedrich)
> But you won't leave me behind.

They smile at each other.

> FRIEDRICH
> No, indeed. Any suitors?

> ELISABETH
> (disgusted)
> Bah.

AUNT ROSALIE
It seems few men rise to the level of expectation of
our dear Lizzie.

ELISABETH
Most of them are uncultured, uneducated or...

FRANZISKA
...Without sufficient fortune.

They all laugh. Friedrich only picks at his food.

ELISABETH
If they could only be like Fritz.

AUNT ROSALIE
Tell us what you have been learning at the
university, Friedrich.

Friedrich looks at Rosalie. Then Mother. Elisabeth. They wait with wide-eyed
innocence.

FRIEDRICH
I have learned...

He pauses, unsure whether to go on. Then with resolve...

FRIEDRICH
That we have been misled for two thousand years
by an illusion.

The women are not quite sure what to make of it.

FRIEDRICH
Of the two great European narcotics, alcohol and
Christianity...

Elisabeth sets her glass of wine down like a hot potato.

FRIEDRICH
...Christianity is the one great curse -- The one
immortal blemish of mankind.

They all freeze in shock, unable to believe their ears.

Friedrich is relieved. He takes a happy bite of food.

FRANZISKA

Son!

AUNT ROSALIE

That's blasphemy!

FRIEDRICH

Amen.

And he finally eats with content.

FRANZISKA

Oh, dear Lord.

Franziska begins to cry.

ELISABETH

How can you say such things, Friedrich? God is
the source of all happiness.

FRIEDRICH

Is that what you want -- happiness? Very well
then, believe. Do you want truth? Then doubt.

Franziska's crying increases to weeping.

FRANZISKA

Oh, dear Lord!

Franziska leaves the table in tears. Rosalie follows dutifully.

Elisabeth turns to Friedrich in anger.

ELISABETH

Look what you've done.

Shame overcomes Friedrich. He sighs deeply.

EXT. NAUMBURG, CHURCH GRAVEYARD - DAY

Friedrich and Elisabeth walk up to the churchyard on the hill, leading a horse by
the reins.

Friedrich releases the horse and hits its flank. It trots around the field. They stand
amidst a host of gravestones and marble. Elisabeth stands defiantly with her
back to him.

ELISABETH

I've worshipped you. And now, you reward me
with this? And on the holy day of Easter no less.

(beat)

I'm ashamed of you.

FRIEDRICH

(unashamed)

I'm sorry, Elisabeth.

ELISABETH

You should apologize to mother.

FRIEDRICH

It's not you - or her - I reject.

ELISABETH

It might as well be.

She holds out a crucifix on a necklace, the one she gave him.

ELISABETH

You put this on my pillow. I gave it to you.

She throws the crucifix to the ground in anger.

And then starts to FAINT. Friedrich catches her. She winces in melodramatic
indecision.

FRIEDRICH

Elisabeth. I must be true to myself. I must become
who I am.

ELISABETH

(not following)

You'll scandalize our family name.

Friedrich releases her. Now he won't look at her.

ELISABETH

You've become so -- so hard.

Friedrich starts to respond, thinks better, starts over.

> FRIEDRICH
>
> It's true, I've changed. But I'm still the same
> person. I'm still your brother.

Elisabeth's heart bleeds for him.

> ELISABETH
>
> Oooh. -- Fritz! Very well. I don't understand why
> you've done what you've done. But you are my
> brother. I love you. And that will never change.

Friedrich smiles, remembers an oath so very long ago. Holds his heart, raises his hand in playful memory.

> FRIEDRICH
>
> "I will live forever and only for my darling sweet
> brother."

He looks at her, waiting. She smiles broadly.

> ELISABETH
>
> SOURPUSS BROTHER.

They laugh and hug.

> FRIEDRICH
>
> My faithful Llama.

They embrace. Friedrich appears sadly detached.

> NARRATOR (V.O.)
>
> He saw at that moment that his mother and sister
> must be his enemies. If his sister would seek the
> impossible task of reconciling darkness and light,
> love and hatred -- Then he would oblige her.

Elisabeth pulls back and smiles with delight.

Friedrich hides the fact that he doesn't share her self-deception.

INT. TRAVELLING TRAIN - DAY

BACK TO THE PRESENT. 63-year old Overbeck still in the traveling train. He puts Nietzsche's letters away and closes his briefcase. Stares out the window.

NARRATOR (V.O.)
But what is worse? To believe a lie, or to live one?

INT. APARTMENT HALLWAY, BASEL UNIVERSITY - DAY

SUPER: Basel University, Switzerland - 1869

FRIEDRICH, NOW 26, still well-dressed as always, struggles with a large trunk and several boxes at his apartment door. His mustache is a bit more grown in. He's not very healthy.

Behind him is a flustered ELISABETH, NOW 24. She's attractive, ladylike, with a touch of pedigree. Though she is a bit uptight, you can't help but like her.

YOUNG OVERBECK, NOW 33, walks into the hallway and notices the two of them. They look up.

OVERBECK
Need some help?

Friedrich sighs apologetically.

FRIEDRICH
Books. A heavy load. But worth the weight.

OVERBECK
I'm Franz Overbeck.

FRIEDRICH
Friedrich Nietzsche.

Overbeck stops with sudden awareness. Friedrich nods to Elisabeth who whisks into the apartment.

FRIEDRICH
My sister, Elisabeth.

ELISABETH
I hope this dingy cage has a proper water closet.

She finds it and enters it. Overbeck helps him lift the trunk into the apartment.

OVERBECK
University of Leipzig doctorate, professor of
philology without examination or dissertation.
Your reputation precedes you.

Friedrich is embarrassed.

> OVERBECK
>
> Don't be ashamed. That's quite an achievement.
> Welcome to Basel University, Herr Professor.

Friedrich smiles. Opens his trunk and unloads books.

> FRIEDRICH
>
> If it weren't for the stench of Luther and Calvin.

> OVERBECK
>
> Ah, yes. Festering breeding ground of the
> Reformation.

> FRIEDRICH
>
> And your post?

> OVERBECK
>
> Professor of New Testament Literature.

> FRIEDRICH
> (horrified)
> I'm sorry. I didn't realize...

> OVERBECK
>
> It's quite alright, really. Actually, I'm an atheist.

Overbeck smiles at Friedrich's surprise.

> OVERBECK
>
> I teach religious literature because I have no other
> skill worthy of income.

> FRIEDRICH
>
> That's quite a contradiction to be living.

> OVERBECK
>
> I wouldn't call it a contradiction. I would call it --
> subversion.

Friedrich smiles. They've connected.

> OVERBECK
>
> Tell a soul and I'll deny all.

Just then, Elisabeth exits the water closet and joins in.

> ELISABETH
> Well, Mr. Overbeck, I understand Basel to be a
> fine school of religion.

Overbeck glances subtly at Friedrich who looks wryly back.

> OVERBECK
> Indeed, it is.
> > (to Friedrich)
> > If there's anything I can help you with, just let me
> > know.
> > (to Elisabeth)
> > It was a pleasure meeting you, Fräulein Nietzsche.
> > Friedrich.

Elisabeth nods aristocratically. Overbeck leaves.

> ELISABETH
> What a nice Christian gentleman.

Friedrich smiles to himself and continues to unload books.

INT. OVERBECK'S BASEL CLASSROOM - DAY

Overbeck enters with his attaché case and stops. Only five students in the chairs.
It's dark, depressing.

He takes the podium. In a dry academic monotone, he begins.

> OVERBECK
> Let's open our books to Chapter four: Faith and
> Reason.

The students dutifully, boringly obey.

> OVERBECK
> We will begin reading from page sixty three...

INT. FRIEDRICH'S BASEL CLASSROOM - DAY

Friedrich looks out over his mere group of eight students in a dreary classroom.
He peers with disgust at the textbook. Slams it shut. Shoves it back into his
attaché case.

He writes two words on the board: APOLLO and DIONYSUS.

> FRIEDRICH
> Apollo and Dionysus. The two poles of all
> philosophy -- of all life. The eternal struggle of
> opposites. Apollo: reason, logic, death. Dionysus:
> passion, spirit, LIFE.

The students are taken aback by their teacher's zeal. And his dramatic fervor increases. A man possessed by his ideas.

(NOTE: As he continues, his dashing clothes change with each shot and the audience increases through time lapse dissolves. Even the room gets brighter with light.)

> FRIEDRICH
> Like the Greeks, we use our rationality to restrain
> our innermost desires. This is Apollo.

OVERBECK'S CLASS

Overbeck writes, "Chapter Three" on the blackboard. He turns to his podium to find his place in the book. His students fight staying awake.

FRIEDRICH'S CLASS

His intensity escalates. His audience is larger.

> FRIEDRICH
> But the wild abandon, the chaos we suppress, this
> is Dionysus.

A student raises his hand. Friedrich calls on him.

> STUDENT
> But -- how does this relate to us?

Friedrich gives the student a condescending look. He crosses out the word "APOLLO" on the board and writes in its place, "CHRIST."

It dawns on the student. Friedrich continues.

> FRIEDRICH
> Philosophy is tragedy. The philosopher, a tragic
> hero, who because he understands the nature of

reality, lives above society's norms. He draws
scandal to himself and is therefore destined by the
gods to suffer for his originality...

OVERBECK'S CLASS

Overbeck paces the floor, book in hand, pausing thoughtfully, considering what to say. There are only five students.

FRIEDRICH'S CLASS

Friedrich doesn't pace, he dances. And he delivers like an operatic libretto. It's standing room only now. In the back of the room, a gawky-looking DEAN peers in, observing.

> FRIEDRICH
> But through the tragic hero's suffering and misery,
> he spreads a magical blessing that extends far
> beyond his own death. And this is his
> resurrection!

OVERBECK'S CLASS

It's down to two students. They are taking writing tests.

Overbeck fights staying awake. He turns to look at the door. The gawky Dean is there. Overbeck gets up to talk to him.

> FRIEDRICH (V.O.)
> There must be violence. There must be suffering
> and pain in order to build the foundation of a new
> world upon the ruins of the old!

FRIEDRICH'S CLASS

Friedrich's fevered pitch is out of control. He suddenly stops himself. The students are confused but amused. But one of them is sleeping.

> FRIEDRICH
> We must annihilate. We must philosophize with a
> hammer!

Friedrich takes a big book and SLAMS it loudly on the desk. The sleeping student wakes up, disoriented.

> FRIEDRICH
> Herr Kaufmann. Would you please explain for us
> Thomas Aquinas' cosmological argument for the
> existence of God.

The student is dumbfounded. He's obviously slept through too many classes. He glances around nervously. Doesn't know what to say. Students CHUCKLE.

Friedrich paces up front and MUMBLES agreement as if listening intently to an answer. Embarrassing tension grows.

Finally, Friedrich gestures at Kaufmann for the class.

> FRIEDRICH
> (sarcastic)
> Ladies and gentlemen. Behold, the power of
> Christian rationality.

The Students LAUGH. Kaufmann slides down in his seat, humiliated.

Friedrich holds a migraine attack at bay.

INT. OVERBECK'S APARTMENT, BASEL UNIVERSITY - NIGHT

Overbeck is writing. He hears a LOUD CRASH through the wall. Books tumbling. And a final SCREAM of resignation.

He gets up and walks out his door into...

INT. HALLWAY

He knocks on Friedrich's door. Opens it.

There at his desk is Friedrich, rubbing his eyes under his reading glasses, a pile of books at his feet.

> OVERBECK
> Friedrich? Are you well?

Friedrich has a glazed look. Did he hear him? Overbeck sees a paper in Friedrich's hand. It's sheet music.

> OVERBECK
> You're a composer?

> FRIEDRICH
> (pulling himself together)
> Just a hobby.

> OVERBECK
> Well. A man of many talents.
> (noting Friedrich's clothes)
> And a keen sense of fashion. That's ironic. -- Let's
> go for a walk. Swiss air will clear your mind.

EXT. BASEL CAMPUS - NIGHT

Friedrich and Overbeck walk along the campus. Overbeck pulls out a cigar, offers it to Friedrich.

> OVERBECK
> Smoke?

> FRIEDRICH
> No, thank you. Makes me nauseous.

> OVERBECK
> No cigars, no beer, wine or coffee.

> FRIEDRICH
> Asceticism is not my cross to bear by choice. It's
> divine revenge.

Overbeck is amused.

> OVERBECK
> The tragic hero rises from within, his individuality
> borne on the wings of his own despair. Fait
> accompli!

It brings a smile to Friedrich's face.

> FRIEDRICH
> Tell me, Franz, what is your fate?

Overbeck looks at him, amused.

                    OVERBECK
          A quiet life of reason and scholarship -- without
          suffering and pain.

Friedrich snickers.

                    OVERBECK
          I have no pretensions of "turning the world
          upside down," if that's what you mean. I prefer
          the quiet assurance of reason to the dangerous
          chaos of passion. And you?

                    FRIEDRICH
          I want to turn the world upside down.

Overbeck smiles.

                    FRIEDRICH
          I'm serious.

                    OVERBECK
          Indeed. And it seems the faculty has caught wind
          of your desire and are none too happy for it.

                    FRIEDRICH
          Cowards. I don't care what they think. I'm in a
          battle of wills with God. He made me an orphan.
          So, I vowed that one day, I would return him the
          favor.
                    (beat)
          Overbeck, I'm going to destroy Christianity and
          create a new world. A new heaven and earth.

Then Friedrich stops with a stagger of pain.

Overbeck tries to hold him up, but Friedrich keeps him at bay. Then keeps
walking in defiance of his pain.

                    OVERBECK
          A rather tall order for a young philologist with
          migraines and eye strain.

> FRIEDRICH
>
> I know it's absurd. But I feel as if I'm a prophet
> with a mission. A destiny.

> OVERBECK
>
> That's quite a contradiction to be living.

> FRIEDRICH
>
> I wouldn't call it a contradiction. I would call it --
> subversion.

They both smile in union. Friedrich thinks about it.

> FRIEDRICH
>
> And I'll call myself -- "Zarathustra"! Zarathustra,
> the prophet!

> OVERBECK
>
> Well then, "Zarathustra," do you think God is
> going to just stand around and not put up a fight?

> FRIEDRICH
>
> He thinks he can stop me with suffering. Ha! I'll
> crucify him.

INT. TRAIN - DAY

BACK TO THE PRESENT. Overbeck's train has stopped. The WHISTLE BLOWS.
He pulls his bag out and pushes through the crowded aisle.

> NARRATOR (V.O.)
>
> In crucifixion, the criminal is stripped naked in
> humiliation. His hands and feet are nailed to the
> wood...

EXT. BASEL TRAIN STATION

Overbeck jumps off the train. He stops in the midst of the bustling crowd looking
for someone. The TRAIN WHISTLES. Moves on. The people are cleared out and
he stands alone.

> NARRATOR (V.O.)
> ...But he does not die from these wounds. Rather,
> the weight of his body puts pressure on the lungs
> until the victim can no longer breathe. -- And he
> suffocates.

He is brought to by the voice of his wife, Beautiful, loyal IDA OVERBECK. A strong liberated woman who has freely chosen to be a support to her husband.

> IDA
> Franz! Franz!

He looks up and smiles. She runs up to him and they embrace. She looks at him in anticipation.

> OVERBECK
> Ida, my love. Nietzsche is finished.

Her demeanor sullens. She grabs him tightly by the arm and they wander out of the station.

INT. OVERBECK LIVING ROOM - NIGHT

Overbeck sits by the fire with a lamp to light his letters. Ida hands him a cup of tea and he reads.

> NARRATOR (V.O.)
> It would be this friend who would lead him to a
> great man who could turn the world upside down.
> (beat)
> But great men do not turn the world upside down.
> Their disciples do.

FLASHBACK: INT. NIETZSCHE'S BASEL APARTMENT - NIGHT

FRIEDRICH, 26 AGAIN, writes frenetically in his darkened room. He finishes, exhausted. Takes off his glasses.

Pours some drops into his bleary, puffy eyes.

He holds his stomach and grimaces in pain. Looks at the bottle. Guzzles it.

A KNOCK at the door frightens him. He hides the bottle, wipes his eyes and walks to the door.

It's OVERBECK, 33 AGAIN. His smile turns to concern.

> OVERBECK
> You don't look well.

Friedrich turns away, trying to hide it.

> FRIEDRICH
> I asked to be appointed to the open chair of
> philosophy. I was denied.

> OVERBECK
> I'm sorry, Friedrich.

Friedrich turns back in passion toward his friend.

> FRIEDRICH
> Ah. Philosophy isn't everything.
>
>   (suddenly depressed)
> But everything is philosophy.

Overbeck notes with empathy.

> OVERBECK
> I know the sister of a certain hero of yours. And
> she told me that certain someone is in town and
> would like to meet you.

Friedrich's eyes widen in shock, excitement.

> FRIEDRICH
>   No.

Overbeck smiles. Yes.

INT. BROCKHAUS PARLOR - NIGHT

High society types grace the modest parlor of the Basel home.

FRÄU BROCKHAUS, a gossipy high-strung hostess, skitters up to a maid carrying a platter of appetizers. She checks them. Acceptable. The maid moves on. She looks around and fidgets with her uncomfortable bustle.

A KNOCK at the front door. A BUTLER opens wide to reveal Overbeck and Nietzsche, dressed to the hilt.

From a distance, Fräu Brockhaus sees the two enter. She gasps and rushes over.

> FRÄU BROCKHAUS
> Professors Overbeck and Nietzsche! How
> welcome you are!

Fräu Brockhaus looks Friedrich up and down, impressed with his handsomeness and attire.

> OVERBECK
> Thank you, Fräu Brockhaus. It is an honor.

Nietzsche shyly agrees. Fräu Brockhaus looks at Overbeck.

> FRÄU BROCKHAUS
> And how is the work at the school?

> OVERBECK
> Weary and endless. Couldn't be better.

They laugh. But Fräu Brockhaus' laugh is LOUD AND HIDEOUS.

Overbeck glances at Friedrich. Nearby guests stop and look in their direction.

Fräu Brockhaus clumsily shuts up.

> FRÄU BROCKHAUS
> And you, Professor Nietzsche. I hear your lectures
> on Greek tragedy are all the rage.

Friedrich looks embarrassingly at Overbeck.

> FRIEDRICH
> I wouldn't say that too loud.

> FRÄU BROCKHAUS
> (wagging a naughty finger)
> The Master wants to talk to you.
>
> (Friedrich shies)
> I'll introduce you myself.

She leads them like a whirlwind through the crowd.

> FRÄU BROCKHAUS
> Have you seen "the Meistersinger?"

FRIEDRICH
Only fools haven't.

FRÄU BROCKHAUS
(like a whirlwind herself)
It's one of his finest operas. He's working on a
new one. Calls it "The Ring." All about German
mythology. It'll be the grandest opera of them all.
He says it's such a spectacle, they'll have to build
an entire opera house just to perform it.

INT. BROCKHAUS DRAWING ROOM

They whisk into the drawing room filled with socialites.

FRÄU BROCKHAUS
Richard! Richard!

As the three of them enter, a crowd parts and creates a processional line that
leads to the altar of one man and woman:

RICHARD WAGNER AND COSIMA VON BÜLOW. Richard, 55, a small man,
but kingly, has all the charisma of a superstar -- and knows it. He wears an
eccentric Flemish painter's costume: knickers, velvet jacket and Rembrandt beret.

Cosima, his beautiful lavish escort, is grace incarnate, and a good deal taller than
Wagner. At 23 years old, she looks more his daughter than his consort. They are
king and child queen among their adoring subjects.

FRÄU BROCKHAUS
Friedrich Nietzsche and Franz Overbeck, I
introduce you to the Master, Richard Wagner.

The crowd quiets. Friedrich and Overbeck bow. Wagner acknowledges.

Then Friedrich stops in stupefied awe of Cosima's beauty. She smiles back at
him.

WAGNER
So, this is the lad who is causing all the ruckus
with his outdated ideas of tragedy.

Uneasiness sweeps over the crowd. Friedrich is speechless. He looks at Overbeck
and prepares for a lashing.

WAGNER

All I can say is -- It's about time.

Everyone LAUGHS in nervous relief. Fräu Brockhaus' hideous CACKLING hits like a wet rag. Friedrich saves the day.

FRIEDRICH

It is an honor to meet you, Master Wagner -- and your wife.

WAGNER

Oh! Forgive me. This is Fräu Cosima von Bülow.

The crowd shifts uneasily. Faux Pas for Friedrich.

FRIEDRICH

Oh. I'm sorry. I...

The women blush. The men raise their brows and COUGH.

WAGNER

Quite all right. Scandal is my middle name!

The crowd LAUGHS nervously again. Cosima raises her hand for Friedrich to grasp. He does so.

FRIEDRICH

Truly an honor.

Cosima nods in approval. Her glory glows.

WAGNER

My dear boy, in this monogamous part of the world, to marry means to split one's rights in half and to double one's duties. So why should I?

Friedrich looks up at Wagner in great interest.

FRIEDRICH

Schopenhauer.

WAGNER

Why, yes. You read Schopenhauer?

FRIEDRICH

Read him? I worship him.

Wagner is intrigued.

> WAGNER
> I know him. You and I have much to talk about.

Friedrich's eyes are wide with delight. Cosima smiles.

> WAGNER
> But not here.
> (leans in close to whisper)
> Not among these peasants. You'll come to
> Tribschen.

Friedrich is pleased. Overbeck shares his joy.

> WAGNER
> I almost forgot.

He turns to one of his escorts and grabs some papers that he gives to Friedrich
and Overbeck. They are signed portraits of himself. Wagner grins.

INT. NIETZSCHE BASEL APARTMENT - DAY

Elisabeth puts down the photograph of Wagner and ties Friedrich's necktie
properly, which is unnecessary because he dresses better than she does. He is
carefully quiet.

> ELISABETH
> The Great Richard Wagner. Too great for your
> inconsequential little sister who came all the way
> from Naumburg.
> (he won't respond)
> The Master receives a new disciple! No women
> allowed.

> FRIEDRICH
> Elisabeth.

> ELISABETH
> Well. Why can't I come?

> FRIEDRICH
>
> You'll be at the Webers right across the lake. I'll pick you up afterwards.

> ELISABETH
>
> He should know that you and I are inseparable!

> FRIEDRICH
>
> Once he gets to know me, I'm sure he won't mind you coming along.

> ELISABETH
>
> Master Wagner, this is my horse, my dog, and oh yes, my sister Elisabeth. You don't mind if she "comes along," do you? I'll keep her on a leash.

> FRIEDRICH
>
> That's not what I meant, Elisabeth. Although the leash isn't a bad idea.

He smiles. She breaks down and smiles.

And then his door opens to Overbeck, dressed up and ready to go.

EXT. TRIBSCHEN - DAY

The carriage arrives at Wagner's Tribschen mansion. Friedrich and Overbeck gaze in awe as they get out of the carriage.

EXT. WEBER'S HOME ACROSS THE LAKE - DAY

Elisabeth stands on the back porch of the Weber's home. In the distance, she sees Friedrich and Overbeck approach the mansion.

She sits down in frustration. Looks over and sees a telescope on the porch pointing to the heavens.

She smiles, gets up and tilts the telescope down to earth -- right at the Wagner's home. She puts her eye to it, focuses.

EXT. TRIBSCHEN VERANDA

Wagner, Cosima, Friedrich and Overbeck are waiting to be served their dinner at an elaborately decorated table. They all laugh. Wagner is in control.

>   WAGNER
> "Germany for Germans," that's what I said.
>
>   (a melodramatic pause)
> The Fatherland is unified. The German spirit is
> invincible!
>
>   FRIEDRICH
> They say war is brewing on the horizon again.
> This time with France.
>
>   WAGNER
> Let it! We'll crush the Frogs. We'll eat them for
> dessert!

More laughter. A servant sets the platter down in front of Friedrich. The lid is pulled off. It's a roasted pig, head and all.

Friedrich goes nauseous. Wagner notices.

>   WAGNER
> You're not -- a Semite?
>
>   FRIEDRICH
> Oh, no, Master. I'm vegetarian for a troubled
> stomach.
>
>   WAGNER
> Bah! Meat makes a mensch. We'll make a
> carnivore out of you yet, Friedrich.

Friedrich fakes a smile to Overbeck as the servant moves the platter in front of Wagner.

>   WAGNER
> You know, Friedrich, I like you. You're passionate.

Friedrich lights up with adoration.

>   WAGNER
> Unlike our friend, Overbeck here. So cool and
> composed. So, content with his -- rationality.

Overbeck yields with a content shrug.

                    WAGNER
But you. You're dissatisfied. You're a wild stallion.
I like that.

Cosima likes this too.

                    FRIEDRICH
Thank you, Herr Meister. You have been an
inspiration.

                    WAGNER
How would you like to be my disciple?

This shocks Friedrich. Impresses Overbeck. Delights Cosima.

                    WAGNER
My destiny is to recreate man through music. New
myths, a new German spirit. I call it, "Music of the
future." A zeitgeist that is not held down by the
chains of petty Christian dogma.

                    COSIMA
Richard.

                    WAGNER
Sorry, dear.
        (back to Friedrich)
A point of constant tension between us. My dear
consort holds tenaciously to her Protestant beliefs.

Cosima sits proud.

                    WAGNER
Except of course, for that annoying little command
against adultery.

Cosima slaps him. He laughs with Friedrich and Overbeck.

                    WAGNER
Well, how about it? I need a writer. Someone who
can publish to the world abroad my...
        (searching)
Well -- my greatness.

Everyone laughs. Friedrich is a bit tongue-tied.

> FRIEDRICH
> Ah -- I -- It would be an honor, Herr Meister.

> WAGNER
> Good. Good.

Friedrich gets an idea. He stands up like a mighty opera singer, and with operatic excess he hams it up and sings:

> FRIEDRICH
> (looking at Cosima)
> To thee, Venus, goddess of love,
> shall my song ring out!
> Now let thy praise be sung aloud by me!
> Thy honeyed fascination is fount of all beauty,
> and every sweet wonder stems from thee!

Cosima is flattered by his attention. In their eyes, a connection. But Cosima breaks it with a look at Wagner.

Wagner is oblivious to it, caught up in his own glory.

But Overbeck catches it.

Everyone applauds as Friedrich bows. Cosima claps the loudest and longest.

> COSIMA
> Wonderful! Wonderful!

> FRIEDRICH
> Opera Tannhauser by Master Richard Wagner.

> WAGNER
> My Nietzsche, your devotion is truly touching. I
> consider you like a son.

Everyone is impressed. Friedrich gulps with a dry throat.

IN HIS MIND'S EYE, he sees Wagner as his father, Karl. But then Wagner's punchline brings him back into reality.

> WAGNER
> But I have to say, you had best stick to prose. I'll
> take care of the opera.

Everyone LAUGHS. Friedrich looks at Wagner, back in reality, but renewed with hope.

> NARRATOR (V.O.)
> And so, a disciple was born. A destiny forged. A
> journey begun for Zarathustra the prophet.

ELISABETH'S TELESCOPIC POV

Across the lake, Elisabeth sees Friedrich amidst the laughter. He stands there like a kid wanting more.

> ELISABETH
> Oh, Fritz. You're making a fool of yourself. Sit
> down. Sit down.

Finally, he sits down. Elisabeth pulls away from the telescope.

> ELISABETH
> Oh, dear brother, what would you do without
> your faithful Llama?

INT. FRIEDRICH'S CLASSROOM - DAY

A cold winter. The room is packed with students. They're in mid-laughter at something Friedrich has said.

But Friedrich changes abruptly to dead seriousness. He holds their attention like a god orating from Olympus.

> FRIEDRICH
> Don't miss the point. The philosopher must take
> his stand beyond good and evil and leave the
> illusion of morality behind. Religious guilt,
> nationalistic pride, must all be overcome. Man
> must himself be overcome.

The students SNICKER. Friedrich is interrupted by the gawky-looking Dean from earlier at his doorway.

INT. DEAN'S OFFICE - DAY

Friedrich sits uneasily at a large table in a dark Dean's office.

On the other side of the table sit SIX DEANS, including the gawky-looking one. It looks like some kind of court session. And Friedrich is the defendant. But no one is speaking, just staring at Friedrich.

The door bursts open to a panting Overbeck, who has rushed over to be here.

> GAWKY DEAN
>
> Professor Overbeck! Welcome. Please take a seat.

The Dean gestures to an open chair on the Dean's side. Overbeck looks suspiciously at the set up. Walks over and stands next to Friedrich instead.

> GAWKY DEAN
>
> Well, we were, ah, just speaking to Professor Nietzsche here about his rather - unorthodox - method of teaching.

An old Curmudgeon of a Dean speaks up.

> CURMUDGEON DEAN
>
> More like fanaticism.

> OVERBECK
>
> Just what exactly is Friedrich's crime that requires such an Inquisition?

> GAWKY DEAN
>
> Herr Professor, this is not a trial. We are only concerned with the reputation of this fine university.

> OVERBECK
> (sarcastic)
> Oh, of course.

> GAWKY DEAN
>
> It appears Friedrich is quite - popular - among the students with his - anti-religious emphasis.

> OVERBECK
>
> With which most of you agree.

GAWKY DEAN

Yes, but... this is drawing attention from the
society at large. I'm sure we all agree that society
requires a certain "ignorance" to maintain its
stability.

Friedrich finally speaks up with the courage of a Socrates.

FRIEDRICH

So, what you are saying is, you want to change the
hearts and minds of our students, but you are too
dishonest to admit it to those who hold your purse
strings because you fear their reprisal.

The Deans look at one another, dead in their tracks.

Overbeck sits down, a little scared by Friedrich's audacity.

FRIEDRICH

Gentlemen. You are the trouble with this
institution. Scholars have become whores for the
highest bidder. I hold the future of humanity in
the palm of my hand. Good day.

Friedrich leads Overbeck out. The Deans glare at the Curmudgeon Dean.

CURMUDGEON DEAN

Stop glaring at me!

EXT. CITY OF NAUMBURG - DAY

It's snowing out. The storefronts are decorated for Christmas. People bustle up
and down the cobbled streets preparing for the holidays.

Friedrich, Overbeck and Elisabeth walk down the avenue all bundled up.

ELISABETH

Oh, Fritz, I'm so excited about tonight. I'm finally
going to meet the Master, and we'll be one big
family. The Nietzsche-Wagners! Aristocrats!

Friedrich has his own fantasy.

FRIEDRICH

Master and disciple -- father and son -- we'll
become -- our own destiny!

Elisabeth pulls him closer in proud affection.

ELISABETH

I always knew you would bring greatness to the
Nietzsche family.

FRIEDRICH

And Cosima -- the Unique! Such a thing of beauty.

Elisabeth pulls away from him. Joy turns suspect.

ELISABETH

That's his wife, Fritz, not his daughter.

FRIEDRICH

Yes, well.

ELISABETH

Of course, she could have fooled me.

Friedrich glances at Overbeck. Elisabeth misses it. She pulls him into a
merchant's store. Overbeck follows.

EXT. TRIBSCHEN MANSION - NIGHT

Friedrich helps Elisabeth get off their carriage and into the cumbersome snow.
Overbeck trails obediently behind. They're all dressed for a dinner occasion.

They walk up to the mansion entrance. The door knocker is a big Golden "W."
Friedrich reaches for it. Pauses. Pulls back.

FRIEDRICH

Elisabeth, I need to tell you something.

She looks innocently at him. Overbeck stands back.

FRIEDRICH

I didn't tell you earlier, but you need to know that
-- uh --

He glances at Overbeck, who looks away.

> FRIEDRICH
>
> Richard and Cosima are not married.

Elisabeth GASPS in horror.

> FRIEDRICH
>
> Yet! - That is, -- they will be.
> -- I think.

> ELISABETH
>
> You think? You think?!
>
> > (she turns to Overbeck)
>
> Did you know about this?

Overbeck simpers a "yes" nod.

> ELISABETH
>
> You didn't tell your own sister? But you told this -
> - this -- Colleague!

> FRIEDRICH
>
> I'm sorry, Lisbeth.

> ELISABETH
>
> Is there anything else you haven't told me that
> may just perhaps prevent me from being the total
> and utter fool that you can make of me?

> FRIEDRICH
>
> Well...

> ELISABETH
>
> At least they don't have any children.

> FRIEDRICH
>
> She's pregnant with his child.

Elisabeth almost falls over in a faint.

> ELISABETH
>
> Oh, dear God!

The door opens to Richard and a very pregnant Cosima.

> WAGNER
>
> Friedrich! Overbeck! What the hell are you doing
> just standing there? The butler heard voices.

Friedrich and Elisabeth look at each other.

> COSIMA
>
> This must be your adoring sister! We've waited so
> long to meet you.

Elisabeth forces her smile with a side glance to Friedrich.

> COSIMA
>
> Friedrich never stops praising you in our
> presence!

> ELISABETH
> (barely holding back)
> Oh, my brother is too kind. Too kind.

They all enter, Overbeck hanging safely back out of the way.

INT. TRIBSCHEN ENTRANCEWAY

The entranceway has marble floors. Wall-to-ceiling windows. A huge sweeping
staircase. Cosima pulls Elisabeth aside.

> COSIMA
>
> Friedrich tells me you've simply been dying to see
> Tribschen.

Elisabeth pours on the politeness with all her effort.

> ELISABETH
>
> Indeed.

> COSIMA
>
> Well, let me give you the grand tour. Consider it
> your own home.

Elisabeth glances over at Friedrich with panic.

Wagner pulls Friedrich in the opposite direction.

> WAGNER
>
> Friedrich, I have something I want to show you.

Overbeck is left standing alone.

> WAGNER
>
> Overbeck! You too.

Overbeck smiles and dashes off after them.

INT. TRIBSCHEN STAIRCASE

Cosima leads Elisabeth up the sweeping staircase.

> COSIMA
>
> I've waited so long to meet you. I know we'll be
> just like sisters.

Elisabeth secretly rolls her eyes.

5-year old precocious princess ISOLDE runs up to the top of the stairs.

> ISOLDE
>
> Mommy, mommy!

> COSIMA
>
> Isolde, I want you to meet your Auntie Elisabeth.

Elisabeth looks shocked at Cosima.

Isolde runs up to Elisabeth and hugs her ferociously. Elisabeth is a statue. She doesn't know how to respond.

> ISOLDE
>
> Hello, Auntie Elisabeth.

With frigid resignation, she pats the little bastard.

> COSIMA
>
> Come along, come along.

INT. TRIBSCHEN DRAWING ROOM

Wagner, Friedrich and Overbeck stand around a covered model.

> WAGNER
>
> Gentlemen. Gaze upon the dawning of a new era.
> The realization of the German Spirit! Bayreuth!

He pulls the cover off. It's an architectural model of a huge opera house. Bold, gaudy and self-aggrandizing.

> OVERBECK
>
> It's incredible.

> FRIEDRICH
> (put off)
> A monument to your grandeur, Master.

> WAGNER
>
> My operas are far too important to house in the petty bourgeois shacks of the common man.

> OVERBECK
>
> Forgive me for my impertinence, Master, but isn't the common man the audience for your operas?

> WAGNER
>
> Overbeck, we are gods. We create the common man.

Overbeck glances at Friedrich with subtle shock.

> OVERBECK
>
> What does "mad King Ludwig" think about financing such an -- edifice?

> WAGNER
>
> He may be insane, but he knows good opera.

> FRIEDRICH
>
> Why Bayreuth? Why not Berlin or Munich?

Wagner leans close in a conspiratorial hush.

> WAGNER
>
> Jews, Friedrich. Semites have spoiled the beauty that was once Berlin.

Overbeck looks away in revulsion. Did he just hear that?

Nietzsche is speechless.

Wagner pulls a manuscript out of a drawer and throws it on the table by Nietzsche.

The manuscript's hand-written title reads: "MY LIFE."

> WAGNER
> My autobiography. I'm writing it in secret, and I
> want you, my Nietzsche, to edit it and publish it.

> FRIEDRICH
> (hiding his distaste)
> Master, I'm flattered.

> WAGNER
> But you must promise me to keep it out of the
> hands of Jewish publishers. They -- are not so
> refined in their understanding of Teutonic
> splendor.

Overbeck looks at Friedrich, both, still holding back.

> FRIEDRICH
> (subtly sarcastic)
> We wouldn't want your greatness tainted.

> WAGNER
> I want you to start proofing as soon as you can.

> FRIEDRICH
> That will be difficult.

Friedrich looks at Overbeck. Wagner isn't in on it.

> WAGNER
> Why?

> OVERBECK
> France has declared war on Prussia.

> WAGNER
> So.

> FRIEDRICH
> I've enlisted.

Wagner is clearly disappointed. But brightens up.

> WAGNER
> Well, make Germany proud. Shoot a few Franks in
> the head!

> FRIEDRICH
> I'm afraid I won't be quite so heroic. Because of
> my Swiss citizenship at Basel, I'm restricted to
> medical duty.

And then a SCREAM can be heard from across the house.

> WAGNER
> Cosima!

The three men run out of the room.

INT. TRIBSCHEN STAIRCASE

They run up the staircase. They're greeted at the bedroom door by Elisabeth.

> ELISABETH
> It's time!

> WAGNER
> (looking around)
> Midwife! Midwife!

A rotund little MIDWIFE, carrying rags and a pail comes running.

Elisabeth tries to enter but Wagner holds her back.

> WAGNER
> Lizzie, would you mind watching Isolde?
> Friedrich come with me!

Overbeck stays with Elisabeth. She's jealous at being left out.

Cosima's birthing SCREAMS scare the little girl.

> ISOLDE
> Is mommy going to be all right?

> ELISABETH
> Yes, deary.

They are interrupted by another SCREAM of Cosima.

> ELISABETH
> It's just God's way of giving us the blessing of
> children.

She pulls her along the hallway with Overbeck. Cosima's off-screen GROANS play over their discussion.

> ISOLDE
> Daddy says there is no God.

Elisabeth is horrified. Overbeck avoids her look.

> ISOLDE
> Mommy says there is.

Elisabeth grins victoriously at Overbeck.

> ISOLDE
> But daddy always wins.

Overbeck smirks to himself.

> ELISABETH
> Well, your daddy is wrong.

INT. HORSE CARRIAGE - NIGHT

Elisabeth, Friedrich and Overbeck ride home in silence. Elisabeth looks out the window, pouting.

> ELISABETH
> This is not good for our reputation. A man and
> woman living in sin - birthing a bastard. And
> worse, while she is married to another man!

> FRIEDRICH
> She's divorcing soon.

> ELISABETH
> Why must they defy society so?

FRIEDRICH

Lizzie. Listen to me. There are some men -- great
men -- who simply cannot live by society's herd
morality. They're beyond good and evil. They're
masters. They're -- Overmen.

ELISABETH

I don't understand these beliefs of yours.

FRIEDRICH

I don't expect you to understand them. Just -- trust
me. Have faith in me. My little Llama.

ELISABETH

Oh, Friedrich. You are a man of contradictions.

Elisabeth looks out the window.

Friedrich glances at the ever-silent Overbeck and winks. Overbeck smiles thinly.
Friedrich looks sick to his stomach.

NARRATOR (V.O.)

What his sister did not know was the desire
burning inside of him. A love that could not be
returned. He had to get away -- far away.

INT. GERMAN CATHEDRAL - DAY

A baroque Lutheran cathedral. A huge crowd of Wagnerians fill the pews.
CHURCH ORGAN MUSIC grinds away.

Wagner and Cosima, decked out like a modern Tristan and Isolde in elaborate
wedding attire, stand at the altar with a PRIEST. Wagner is not entirely happy.

Elisabeth and Overbeck sit in the pews. Friedrich is absent.

FRIEDRICH (V.O)

Dear Overbeck, send my congratulations to the
Wagners. And my sorrow, once again, for my
inability to be there for their blessed union...

ECU OF FRIEDRICH'S HANDWRITING A LETTER - DAY

With the sounds of battle in the distance.

FRIEDRICH (V.O)

...I have arrived at the front, and the news is good

for Germany. But I must tell you...

EXT. SMALL BURGHER STREET, FRONTLINES - DAY

Friedrich walks through a small burgher street carrying medical supplies.
Flashes of CANNON FIRE drape the horizon.

FRIEDRICH (V.O)

...While on duty in a small town, I was accosted by

the most incredible vision...

Friedrich stops in the street. He listens. Feels.

SOUND-OVER: "Ride of the Valkyries" by Wagner builds.

A group of horse hoofs RUMBLE through the mud.

Impending fear settles on Friedrich. He looks around.

FRIEDRICH (V.O)

...The very cavalry I trained with happened upon

me in the most unlikely of places...

Friedrich sees the cavalry riding up the street towards him. Closer, closer.
Friedrich goes trance-like.

The cavalry tramples by, sounding their BATTLECRY. A dusty cloud around
them. Power and glory. Friedrich salutes them -- with tears.

FRIEDRICH (V.O.)

...I felt for the first time in my life that the

strongest, noblest will to life does not reside in our

puny struggle to exist.

(beat)

But in the will to power. I longed to jump on a

horse and dash with them into battle and death!...

Friedrich stands there in the street in religious ecstasy.

INT. HOSPITAL WARD - NIGHT

As Friedrich finishes writing, we see that he is bedridden.

> FRIEDRICH (V.O.)
> ...But alas, my frail constitution. I collapsed with
> diphtheria and became a patient in my own
> hospital ward. I'll be home soon and look forward
> to seeing you at Bayreuth. Greet the Master for me
> -- and fair Cosima. She never leaves my thoughts.

Friedrich stops. A NURSE with an amazing resemblance to Cosima approaches.

> NURSE COSIMA
> Friedrich, you must stop your writing and get
> some rest!

Friedrich sees her as Cosima in his own mind.

> FRIEDRICH
> Marry me, Cosima.

> NURSE COSIMA
> Who's Cosima?
>
> (looking at the letter)
> Your wife?

He pulls the letter away from her sight.

> FRIEDRICH
> You are Cosima -- the Unique!

> NURSE COSIMA
> Your sickness is going to your head, Friedrich.
> Now, get some rest.

He watches her walk away. Pulls off his reading glasses. Falls back in bed, exhausted.

EXT. NAUMBURG TRAIN STATION - DAY

The station is crowded. A train arrives with a PIERCING WHISTLE. Elisabeth, Overbeck and Franziska watch the train pull to a stop. People get off.

Overbeck stays behind with Franziska. Elisabeth runs to the doors. She anticipates each soldier getting off to be her Fritz. But none of them are. Franziska begins to worry.

Elisabeth backs up as the last of the soldiers hops off. She peers in the windows. No one left.

She looks back at Franziska with worry. Then back at the empty train. Her hand goes to her mouth in dread.

And then she turns and sees, from out of the thinning crowd, Friedrich in his military uniform carrying his bag. Her fear turns to utter happiness.

She runs into the arms of Friedrich. They hug tightly.

> ELISABETH
> We're together again.

He pulls away. Mother embraces son in delight. Overbeck stands back.

> FRANZISKA
> Friedrich, I prayed for you every day.

Friedrich can only pity his mother. He looks up at Overbeck.

> FRIEDRICH
> Friend.

> OVERBECK
> Friend.

First, they shake hands, then can't help but embrace with a hearty laugh.

Elisabeth grabs Friedrich and hugs him again.

> ELISABETH
> Never leave us again, Fritz.

> FRIEDRICH
> I have to go to Tribschen.

Elisabeth reacts like a jealous little girl.

DISSOLVE TO:

INT. WAGNER'S BEDROOM, TRIBSCHEN - DAY

Cosima packs clothes into a trunk. She flurries around in indecision. Should it be the black gown or the white? Black.

A MAID opens the door.

64

MAID
Madame?

Cosima looks up. Friedrich is at the door, dressed dashingly with a huge smile. Cosima yelps and opens her arms.

He comes running. They hug. Cosima is delighted. Friedrich, painful.

COSIMA
Oh, Friedrich! I missed you dreadfully.

FRIEDRICH
And I, you.

COSIMA
I didn't realize how fond I was of you till I considered the possibility of losing you in that horrible war.

FRIEDRICH
(playfully operatic)
Oh, Cosima. Death could not stop Dionysus!

She throws a pillow at him. They share a chuckle.

COSIMA
From the day you first arrived at Tribschen, I knew there was a connection in spirit between you and Richard. I could feel it myself. And I believe history demands its consummation.

FRIEDRICH
(less operatic, still playful)
The Wagnerian and the Nietzschean. As one. Thus saith the Maestro.

COSIMA
Richard is good to me. But I must confess, sometimes our difference in age -- is a difficulty I gratefully do not share with you.

FRIEDRICH
I understand. With all my soul.

Cosima returns to packing.

> COSIMA
>
> You received my letter about coming to Bayreuth?

> FRIEDRICH
>
> I had to see you before you went.

Cosima packs on innocently.

Friedrich prepares to reveal his love.

She is oblivious. Or is she? He hands her a book.

> FRIEDRICH
>
> I finished my first book. I dedicated it to Richard.
> But in my heart, I was thinking of you.

> COSIMA
>
> How sweet.
>
> (she looks at it)
> "The Birth of Tragedy." Richard will be excited to
> read it. Tragedy is so noble. So -- romantic.

She places the book in her luggage.

> FRIEDRICH
>
> The war made me think. -- It made me acutely
> aware of the desperate urgency of life -- and love.

Cosima stops her packing.

> FRIEDRICH
>
> When two people connect, and they feel the union
> of spirits. But they cannot speak their love for fear
> of discovery.

> COSIMA
>
> (agreeing)
> Tragic.

> FRIEDRICH
>
> We forbid ourselves the dangerous kind. And we
> spend the rest of our lives regretting the slavery of
> our own consciences.

(a deep sigh)
Oh, Cosima. I want to live dangerously.

Cosima stops and looks straight at Friedrich.

COSIMA
That's beautiful, Friedrich.

He stares at her. She looks into his eyes with affection and respect. And totally misses the point.

COSIMA
We have to find you a wife.

She continues to pack. His face drops in despair.

COSIMA
When I get to Bayreuth, I'm going to speak to Richard, and we'll see if we can't arrange a liaison of sorts.

She stops and looks at him with warm motherliness.

COSIMA
You know, a great mind like yours can't change the world unless he has a fine supportive wife behind him -- cleaning up after his messes.

She smiles and keeps packing. Friedrich is hopeless.

NARRATOR (V.O.)
"Selfless love is a deception. One always wants to possess the beloved. Even God becomes terrible when one does not love him in return." Thus saith Zarathustra.

INT. FRIEDRICH'S BASEL ROOM - DAY

Friedrich packs his bags. Overbeck looks on, smoking a cigar.

OVERBECK
You've told no one else.

FRIEDRICH
I may detest society, but I'm not suicidal.

OVERBECK

You have a family you cannot avoid. Follow a man you cannot respect. And love a woman you cannot have.

Friedrich stops for a moment. Overbeck is right.

OVERBECK

That's quite a contradiction to be living.

FRIEDRICH

At least I don't follow a religion I cannot believe.

Overbeck is pierced. Friedrich turns passionate.

FRIEDRICH

Why don't you stand up? The world is looking for a god. Someone to lead the way to freedom.

OVERBECK

I'm not interested in martyrdom, Friedrich.

FRIEDRICH

No. You're interested in survival. So you perpetuate the lie.

An uncomfortable silence. Then...

OVERBECK

I'm marrying a woman I met named Ida. We're moving to Eulerstrasse.

This stops Friedrich in surprise.

FRIEDRICH
(sarcastic)
Well, God bless you, Overbeck.

OVERBECK

Will you write?

FRIEDRICH

That's about all I can do.

Friedrich slams his bag shut. Latches it. Walks out the door, leaving Overbeck alone with his thoughts.

EXT. BAYREUTH FESTIVAL HOUSE - DAY

The town is alive with commerce. Merchants' stores are full and peasants carry bread, wood and tools through the streets.

At the top of the hill is the Festival House, realized from Wagner's architectural model. Though incomplete, it's outrageous and overwrought, a monument to a single man's vanity. A Victorian castle towering over its poor subjects.

INT. BAYREUTH FESTIVAL HOUSE - DAY

Inside the opera house, the opening scene from Das Rheingold plays on the cavernous stage. THREE RHINEMAIDENS swimming in the Rhine tease the dwarf ALBERICH. Small bodies, big voices.

Alberich gropes for them. But they dance around him, erotically out of reach. They offer him the Ring and mastery of the world. But there is one caveat. He must give up love. To their surprise, he does -- and takes the Ring...

INT. BAYREUTH FESTIVAL HOUSE ROYAL BOX

Crazy KING LUDWIG of Bavaria sits with his SMALL ENTOURAGE. Next to Ludwig, dressed in aristocratic splendor, is Wagner and Cosima.

Next to them, Elisabeth is eating it all up. Friedrich hardly conceals his disgust with all the pomposity.

EXT. WAGNER RESIDENCE BAYREUTH - NIGHT

A big banner over the large German villa says, "WAHNFRIED."

INT. WAGNER RESIDENCE BAYREUTH - NIGHT

A party is in progress. Guests fill the Wagner home, discussing pleasantries and social norms.

Over in one corner stands the illustrious Richard and Cosima Wagner and their train of worshipping sycophants, among whom is Elisabeth. As Wagner speaks, Elisabeth looks around in search of someone.

> WAGNER
> I tell you, my Nietzsche understands me.
> Understands my deepest vision. And he'll help me
> transform history itself -- if we can only find him a
> wife.
>
> (snickers from the crowd)
> This is his sister, Elisabeth.

He points to Elisabeth. She nods politely.

A big man with a burly mustache, looking somewhat like Friedrich, stands next to her, eyeing her up and down. This is BERNHARD FÖRSTER, adventurer, activist, anti-Semite.

> WAGNER
> But remember! He needs good healthy German
> stock. No Jewry.

The crowd LAUGHS. Förster raises his wine in agreement.

Around the corner, Friedrich pulls back out of view into another room, disgusted by the display.

> FRIEDRICH
> Cultural philistine. Unbridled despot.

He sees a group of academic types whispering scandal amongst themselves -- looking and pointing straight at him.

Suddenly, a man appears from behind. PAUL RÉE, late 20s, suave, smooth intellect. He's an intellectual like Overbeck, but debonair and "devil-may-care."

> RÉE
> Losing your faith in the Master?

Friedrich is startled, then suspicious. Rée looks around the corner at Wagner.

> RÉE
> Didn't you write, "that man to whom, as my
> sublime predecessor, I dedicate this essay on
> Tragedy"?

> FRIEDRICH
> Did I write that?

Rée smiles slyly. He notices the gossiping group.

> FRIEDRICH
> I'll have to change it.

> RÉE
> Me? I think he would slay the German spirit for
> the German Reich.

Friedrich is amused.

> FRIEDRICH
> German Spirit. There's a contradiction in terms.
> And where do you put your faith?

> RÉE
> Certainly not in God. And certainly not in
> anything external to myself.
>
> > (holds out his hand, smiles)
>
> Paul Rée.

Friedrich obliges with cautious interest.

> RÉE
> Herr Nietzsche, you're quite the scandal. New
> morality and all that.

They glance at the whisperers, still gossiping.

> FRIEDRICH
> Yes, well, to my students, I'm a god. To the Deans,
> I'm the devil himself.

> RÉE
> Well then, I guess you don't exist on both
> accounts.

Friedrich looks at him amused. They LAUGH.

An old Kaiser-supporting CODGER breaks out of the whispering academics and trudges up to them. He stares at Friedrich.

> CODGER
> Nietzsche?

> FRIEDRICH
>
> Yes?

The Codger points a bony finger at Friedrich.

> CODGER
>
> Antichrist!

The chattering around them comes to a halt. Friedrich glances around. Everyone stares at him. His head spins.

> CODGER
>
> Nietzsche is Antichrist!

With that, the old Codger walks bitterly away.

> RÉE
>
> Well God bless your Christian charity, old man.

The people nearby distance themselves like he was a leper.

The gossip returns. Mutterings of "atheist" and "god-hater." Friedrich is unshaken.

> RÉE
>
> Pious frauds.

> FRIEDRICH
>
> They're actually afraid of me. They know my
> ideas are going to demolish their miserable little
> universe.

> RÉE
>
> So they'd like to crucify you -- just like they did
> Christ.

Friedrich looks at him. Rée grins slyly. Friedrich grins back. These two are hitting it off.

INT. DRAWING ROOM

Elisabeth is with Förster. The Wagner crowd dispersed. He is enamored with her.

She watches Friedrich and Rée through the hallway.

FÖRSTER

So your brother needs a wife, yet you appear to be here alone.

ELISABETH

Gentlemen are not a high priority for me.

FÖRSTER

For such a distinguished and handsome woman as yourself, I should think deciding suitors would be a full-time endeavor.

ELISABETH

(amused)

I have enough to concern myself with, Herr...

FÖRSTER

Förster. Bernhard Förster.

He clicks his heels and grabs her hand with suave tenderness.

ELISABETH

Herr Förster. I appreciate your compliment, but like my brother and the Master, I am more concerned about the new world that they are both trying to bring about.

FÖRSTER

Wonderful!

This surprises Elisabeth.

FÖRSTER

I share those dreams with you all!

He reaches in his vest and pulls out an Iron Cross hanging on his chest.

FÖRSTER

Forgive my vanity, Miss Nietzsche, but I received this Iron Cross in the war for precisely the same reason. Because I believe that the Fatherland has lost its purity of soil. What we need is a New Germany!

Elisabeth listens with renewed interest.

> FÖRSTER
>
> And I'm going to start it.

Elisabeth can't decide whether she's impressed or humored.

> ELISABETH
>
> Impressive, Herr Förster. But where would you begin this "New Germany"?

> FÖRSTER
>
> Paraguay, South America. The land's cheap.

> ELISABETH
>
> And your citizens?

> FÖRSTER
>
> Volunteers, pioneers, investors -- and my new wife.

> ELISABETH
>
> You are married?

> FÖRSTER
>
> No.

> ELISABETH
>
> Then betrothed.

> FÖRSTER
>
> Seeking.

A spark settles in her eye for the first time in her life.

Friedrich and Rée walk up to Elisabeth.

> FRIEDRICH
>
> Let's go, Elisabeth. I can't take any more of this decadence.

> ELISABETH
>
> Oh, Friedrich. I'm only now beginning to mix. Have you met Herr...

Förster clicks his heels.

>   FÖRSTER

>   FÖRSTER. BERNHARD FÖRSTER.
>   ADVENTURER. EXPLORER.

Friedrich looks him up and down with a shade of contempt.

Förster extends his hand. Friedrich shakes cautiously.

>   FÖRSTER
>   I am a great admirer of your writing, Herr
>   Nietzsche.

Friedrich stares at the fool in silence.

>   FRIEDRICH
>   Congratulations. You're one of the "chosen few."
>   (to Elisabeth)
>   Find your own ride home, then. I'm sickened.

>   FÖRSTER
>   I would be delighted to escort your sister.

>   FRIEDRICH
>   And how do I know I can trust you, Herr...

>   FÖRSTER
>   ...Förster. Bernhard Förster. Because, Herr
>   Nietzsche, I would never dream of violating the
>   valuable treasure of the man who would bring
>   hope to the ancient German spirit.

Friedrich looks nauseated with the flattery.

Elisabeth revels in his jealousy. She slips her arm into Förster's, who is surprised, but delighted.

>   ELISABETH
>   I'll be all right, Fritz.

Friedrich looks spitefully at her embrace.

>   FRIEDRICH
>   So be it.

He leaves with Rée. Elisabeth pats Förster. He likes it.

ELISABETH

He's a bit obtuse when he's not feeling well.

They watch Friedrich and Rée leave.

FÖRSTER

Your brother -- is a great man. Wonderfully
dangerous.

ELISABETH

Yes. Yes, he is.

Elisabeth smirks and glances hungrily at Förster.

INT. HORSE COACH - NIGHT

Friedrich is sickly pale as he rides along with Rée.

RÉE

A prophet is without honor in his own country.

FRIEDRICH

And sick as well. My entire life I've suffered from
an inexhaustible curse of pain. On a constant
search for a milder climate and a few moments of -
- normalcy. The fact of the matter is, Masters do
not change the world. Their disciples do. My
greatest fear is to die without having found a
disciple to help spread my gospel.

Suddenly Friedrich's eyes brighten. He looks at Rée with hopefulness. Rée gulps
with fear.

RÉE

Not me, Plato. I wouldn't last long enough. I'm
suicidal.
(Friedrich sulks)
What about Herr Förster? He seemed to slobber all
over you.

FRIEDRICH

I would wish such disciples on my enemies.

> (mocking voice)
> "You bring hope to the ancient German spirit." --
> Pigheaded bigot.

                    RÉE

Well, he's got a point. Jews are the whiners of the
world.

Friedrich looks at him, surprised. And suspicious.

                    RÉE

Self-loathing. I'm a Jew myself.
> (laughs to himself)
> A living contradiction. A Jewish anti-Semite.

Friedrich smiles with amused relief.

Rée reaches into his pocket. Pulls out a vial of liquid. Caresses it, lovingly.

                    FRIEDRICH

What's that?

                    RÉE

Salvation.
> (Friedrich doesn't get it)
> Potassium cyanide. I carry it with me wherever I
> go. In case the "ever-increasing circle of fanatics"
> closes in too tight, and the impulse to kill myself is
> overwhelming.

Friedrich is open-mouthed in humorous wonder.

                    RÉE

You think I jest.

Rée kisses the vial and puts it away. Friedrich SIGHS.

                    FRIEDRICH

My ideas are enough to get me killed. Or drive me
mad. Whichever comes first.

                    RÉE

Cheer up. The new world is coming. Hell is the
only thing you'll have to worry about.

Friedrich looks at him again. They laugh together. They're becoming fast friends.

> RÉE
> You need to visit me in Italy. Sorrento. It's quiet.
> Clean air. Bring your sister.

Friedrich gives him a sour look.

> RÉE
> Maybe not.
> (beat)
> The women are looser. Who knows? I may even be
> able to help you find a "disciple" among them.

Rée smiles sardonically, amusing Friedrich again.

> FRIEDRICH
> You're a lunatic, Rée.

> RÉE
> Misery loves company.

They exchange smiles.

INT. FRIEDRICH'S BASEL CLASSROOM - DAY

Friedrich is back to teaching his hungry students.

> FRIEDRICH
> To live alone, says Aristotle, one must be an
> animal or a god. But I propose that a philosopher
> is both animal and god.

He falters a bit. A dizzy spell.

> FRIEDRICH
> And I assess the power of his will by how much
> resistance, pain, torture he endures and knows
> how to turn to his advantage.

Another dizzy spell. His vision gets blurry. He has to steady himself. A concerned Student reacts.

> STUDENT
> Herr Professor. Are you well?

Friedrich sits down in his chair to catch his breath, everything still spinning.

INT. DR. BISMARCK'S OFFICE - DAY

Good old burly bearded, one-armed Dr. Bismarck from earlier examines Friedrich's eye. But Bismarck has grayed and now wears coke-bottle glasses himself.

> DR. BISMARCK
> As I thought. You have quite extensive nerve damage, Friedrich. You are almost blind. And the glasses cannot help much.

Friedrich is disappointed at his misfortune.

> DR. BISMARCK
> I recommend no reading or writing for several years.

This hits Friedrich like a millstone.

The Doctor holds out a bottle of medicine to the stone-faced philosopher.

> DR. BISMARCK
> This Chloral is strong, but it will relieve some symptoms.

Then, Friedrich bursts out LAUGHING. Bismarck looks at him like he's a madman.

> FRIEDRICH
> And if I don't stop reading or writing?

> DR. BISMARCK
> More headaches, stomach problems, nausea, less sight, and God knows what other increasing complications with time.

Friedrich puts on his coat and prepares to leave.

> FRIEDRICH
> God knows? Well then, you tell God, doctor, that I will continue to read and write. And I will find a disciple who will help me nail the lid on God's

coffin. And he can just go ahead and keep trying to stop me.

Friedrich slams the door behind him.

INT. DEAN'S OFFICE - DAY

Friedrich sits solemnly with the circle of Deans again. The Gawky Dean leads them.

> GAWKY DEAN
> Friedrich. The board has decided to grant your request for sabbatical leave in light of your health problems. It will be our loss, but we wish you well.

Friedrich gets up and leaves silently. The Codger speaks up.

> CODGER DEAN
> Good riddance! Our Nietzsche problems are finally over. God willing, he won't be able to write with that illness of his.

> ANOTHER DEAN
> Oh, I don't know. The world may not be ready for his ideas now. But one day...

> GAWKY DEAN
> And what will be the consequences?

EXT. SORRENTO RESIDENCE - DAY

Friedrich hops out of a carriage before a large but modest lodge. Rée appears at the door. The two embrace.

Elisabeth looks on jealously from the carriage. Rée takes her hand.

> NARRATOR (V.O.)
> Freedom makes miserable slaves out of men.

INT. FRIEDRICH'S SORRENTO ROOM - NIGHT

Friedrich has trouble reading a manuscript, even with his glasses. He rubs his eyes and hands it back to Elisabeth.

                    FRIEDRICH
Next passage.

                    ELISABETH
You should listen to the doctor, Fritz. I can proof
your manuscript later...

                    FRIEDRICH
Next passage!

                    ELISABETH
          (giving in)
"Selfless love is a deception. One always wants to
possess the beloved. Even God becomes terrible
when one does not love him in return."

                    FRIEDRICH
Stop.

He jots something down. She doesn't like what she reads.

                    ELISABETH
Friedrich, you don't really mean...

                    FRIEDRICH
Yes, Elisabeth, I really mean...

                    ELISABETH
People are not going to approve.

                    FRIEDRICH
I don't care if anyone approves. I am my own
author. I will write my own story. Not you, not
God, not anybody else.

                    ELISABETH
You just aren't yourself these days.

And then a KNOCK on the door.

                    FRIEDRICH
Go away!

                    RÉE (O.S.)
It's Rée.

Friedrich takes off his glasses and rubs his temples.

>FRIEDRICH
>
>All right.

Rée opens the door and saunters in.

>RÉE
>
>Good God, man! No one wants you to stick it to
>those academic bastards more than I. But you can't
>spend your life caged up in a room writing.

>ELISABETH
>
>That's what I keep trying to tell him.

>RÉE
>
>You'll go crazy.
>
>>(Elisabeth nods her head)
>
>Especially with your sister here.

He gives her a teasing smile. She leers at him.

>RÉE
>
>You need some fresh air.

>FRIEDRICH
>
>I suppose you're right.

Rée picks up the manuscript and looks at it.

>RÉE
>
>Damn well. Look at this handwriting. You're all
>ready to be committed.

>ELISABETH
>
>That's my writing!

>RÉE
>
>Whoops. Sorry.

He sets it down like a hot potato. Looks at Friedrich changing the subject.

>RÉE
>
>You know the Wagners will be here tonight.

> ELISABETH
> Here? In Sorrento?

Elisabeth looks at Friedrich who is downcast.

> RÉE
> You're going to tell him, aren't you?

> ELISABETH
> Tell him what?

Elisabeth looks confused between the two. Friedrich sighs.

> ELISABETH
> Tell him what, Friedrich?

She looks to Rée, who shrugs. Then to Friedrich.

> FRIEDRICH
> This is not your business, Elisabeth.

Elisabeth looks at Rée, hiding her hurt.

> ELISABETH
> Your life is my business.

She glances back at Rée. Friedrich stays silent and firm. She's humiliated.

She leaves. Friedrich looks to Rée.

EXT. HALLWAY

Elisabeth pauses in frustration. Storms down the hall.

EXT. SORRENTO RESIDENCE - NIGHT

An elaborate carriage arrives at the Sorrento residence. The horses come to a stop. Richard Wagner looks out.

INT. SORRENTO RESIDENCE WAGNER'S ROOM - LATER

Wagner and Friedrich watch TWO SERVANTS bring in several large trunks. One of them stumbles but catches himself.

> WAGNER
> Be careful! That is an expensive design piece. Put
> it over there.

The servant puts it down and Wagner opens it. Friedrich looks on in silent disgust.

>   WAGNER
>   I read your book, "Human, All Too Human."

Friedrich doesn't respond. The other servant brings in another trunk.

>   WAGNER
>   (to the servant)
>   Over by the bed.
>
>   (to Friedrich)
>   I can see Rée's influence on it.

Wagner walks over to a smaller trunk and unlocks it.

>   WAGNER
>   You really must be careful with this man, Rée. --
>   He is a Semite after all.

>   FRIEDRICH
>   For God's sake, Richard, he's an atheist. And I
>   write my beliefs, not somebody else's.

>   WAGNER
>   All the same. You're my disciple. I'm trying to
>   protect you.

Friedrich grits his teeth, bites his tongue.

Wagner reaches into the trunk and pulls out a manuscript. He tosses it at Friedrich, who catches it.

The servant sets the trunk down and scurries out. Friedrich looks at the manuscript. "MY LIFE" by Wagner.

>   WAGNER
>   I finished it. It's ready for editing.

Friedrich looks at it with trepidation.

>   WAGNER
>   Of course, I'll have to approve all changes as well
>   as publishing rights.

Wagner walks back to the open trunk. Friedrich stares at the book, holding back a volcano of boiling anger.

> WAGNER
> And now, my son, the crowning achievement of
> my career.

He pulls out an elaborate model of the stage setting for the final scene of Parsifal. A small altar with surrounding knight's Roundtable.

> WAGNER
> Parsifal.

He bends down and stares at it, hypnotized by his own glory.

Friedrich stays back in the dark of the room.

> WAGNER
> You can come to Bayreuth and write a pamphlet
> on it. "The spirit of redemption," "the glory of
> myth." Or whatever you like. Of course, I'll expect
> you to bring the biography with you and work on
> it in between.

Friedrich is trying to hold back the mounting fury.

> WAGNER
> Well, what do you think? The Master awaits your
> reply.

And then Friedrich explodes out of the shadows, eyes blazing. He throws the book across the room. It hits the wall, a tangled mess of pages.

Wagner looks at Friedrich with shock.

> FRIEDRICH
> I'll tell you what I think.

He walks up to Wagner and the model, staring madly into Wagner's confused eyes.

> FRIEDRICH
> It's fleshless. It reeks of blood. Christian knights,
> suffering and redemption. Religious clap trap!

Friedrich grabs the model and hurls it against the wall.

> WAGNER
> Friedrich! That is an expensive...

> FRIEDRICH
> Whatever happened to the spirit of greatness that
> you were going to revive in your music? The new
> mythology?

> WAGNER
> You're mad!

> FRIEDRICH
> You talk of Rée infecting me? Look at what
> Cosima has done to you! You're capitulating to
> her -- and her cowardly religion!

> WAGNER
> Why do you have such venom?

> FRIEDRICH
> Because you're a hypocrite! You speak of Christian
> love, yet you hate Jews.

> WAGNER
> They killed the Christ.

> FRIEDRICH
> Christ was a Jew, Richard!

Wagner softens, turns introspective.

> WAGNER
> You are a young man, I am old. Unbelief is no
> longer a luxury for me.

> FRIEDRICH
> Luxury? All you know is luxury. You don't even
> know the meaning of suffering!

> WAGNER
> Maybe not. But God does.

> FRIEDRICH
>
> Ha! Yes, God does indeed know the meaning of
> suffering. In fact, I'd say he glories in the misery of
> his creatures. Schadenfreude. It's a demented form
> of love if you ask me.

> WAGNER
>
> Maybe God isn't asking you, my son. Maybe He's
> telling you.

> FRIEDRICH
>
> Well, you can go tell God, what does not kill me
> makes me stronger.
>
> (beat)
>
> And don't ever call me "son" again. You're not a
> father to me. You never were.

Friedrich suffers a stabbing pain in his head, accented by visionary FLASHES of Friedrich's real father, Karl, in a pose of scorn and indictment. Painful memories.

Wagner moves to help him, but Friedrich pushes him away and continues.

> FRIEDRICH
>
> You're not "The Master." You're a slave. I'm the
> one who needs a disciple. I'm the one who is
> going to rewrite history. I am the future.

Friedrich storms out the door, slamming it behind him. Wagner looks over at his destroyed model and book.

INT. SORRENTO RESIDENCE - NIGHT

It's late. Friedrich sits exhausted and disheveled at his desk chair writing furiously, reading glasses on.

> NARRATOR (V.O.)
>
> And so Zarathustra wrote, "Is madness the true
> purpose of Christian redemption? Is the church
> itself a hospital -- or a madhouse? Is anyone
> actually converted to religion, or is it merely a
> sickness?"

He stops and takes a swig of his medicine. A KNOCK at the door, Rée sticks his head in. Dressed in social attire.

> RÉE
>
> You're still here?

> FRIEDRICH
>
> Do you realize who you are talking to? I am the Prince of Doria!

Rée freezes with caution. Friedrich is acting demented.

> FRIEDRICH
>
> How dare you interrupt my pleasure!

Rée looks for a sign. And then he finds it. An ever-so-slight smirk on Friedrich's mouth. Rée sighs in relief at the joke.

> RÉE
>
> Good God, man. How do you do it?

> FRIEDRICH
>
> I don't know. I suffer for weeks, and then all of a sudden -- I have a reprieve, and I am in a state of -- euphoria. Absolute euphoria -- for days. And my writing -- is as if -- I'm a mere vessel, a tool through which the writing is taking place.

> RÉE
>
> Don't get religious on me.

> FRIEDRICH
> (smiling)
> God forbid.

> RÉE
>
> Say, listen. Tonight, I may have found your salvation.

Friedrich gives him a wry look.

> RÉE
>
> I met a girl that may be the perfect prospect for you.

Friedrich's interest turns to surprise.

> RÉE
> As a disciple.

> FRIEDRICH
> A woman?

> RÉE
> They're not all beasts of burden, you know. Some
> do have intelligence.

> FRIEDRICH
> Well, don't forget the whip.

Friedrich glares at him, and they both break out in LAUGHTER.

INT. HORSE CARRIAGE, ROME - DAY

Friedrich and Rée ride in a jostling carriage. Friedrich looks out the window at the passing Roman architecture. Large marble monuments to man's glory and self-deification.

> NARRATOR (V.O.)
> With Wagner behind him, and all the world before
> him, his search for a disciple would lead him to
> the most invigorating, most inspiring -- and most
> lonely period of his life...

EXT. ST. PETER'S BASILICA, ROME - DAY

Friedrich and Rée step up to the Basilica and look up at its glowering tower. Friedrich wags his head in disgust.

> NARRATOR (V.O)
> He was to meet a woman who would drive him
> mad with desire. A woman he thought he wanted
> more than anything in the world...

INT. ST. PETER'S BASILICA, ROME - DAY

The huge interior rotunda reaches to heaven. Friedrich, stylishly dressed as ever, looks over at Rée, who sits in his pew writing his own manuscript.

Friedrich steps over to an altar lit with a hundred candles. At the apex of it is a painting of Madonna and Child. All the contempt in heaven and earth boil beneath his eyes.

> NARRATOR (V.O.)
> ...A woman he could never have.

> LOU (O.S.)
> Paul!

Friedrich's attention is caught by the whisper. He sees LOU VON SALOMÉ, 21, beautiful and perky, whispering to Rée. She is a vision. A liberated woman, with a soft Russian accent, who is not afraid to exploit her beauty as a means of advancement.

> LOU
> What are you writing?

> RÉE
> A book about the non-existence of God.

> LOU
> (looking around)
> How appropriate.

They look over and see Friedrich.

> RÉE
> Friedrich!

Friedrich glides over.

> RÉE
> I want you to meet Lou von Salomé.

Lou pauses with awe.

> LOU
> How do you do.

Friedrich just stares at her. She smiles. Looks at Rée.

> RÉE
> Friedrich.

And then he speaks as out of a fog.

FRIEDRICH

What stars have sent us orbiting toward each
other?

Lou looks humorously at Rée, then back to Friedrich.

LOU

I've read your writings, Herr Nietzsche.

FRIEDRICH

Dionysus!

LOU

Pardon?

FRIEDRICH

Call me Dionysus!

LOU

The tragic god of passion.

Friedrich's mesmerizing stare turns to smile.

FRIEDRICH

You and I have much to talk about.

Lou smiles back. Then Rée breaks the trance.

RÉE

Well, let's not do it in this tomb!

They all laugh and pick up to leave the cathedral.

EXT. STREET OF ROME, PANTHEON - DAY

Friedrich, Rée and Lou practically run past the obelisk fountain and into the
grand and mythic pantheon.

INT. PANTHEON - DAY

The three of them spin around looking up into the vast rotunda above.

NARRATOR (V.O.)

That day, they traveled the streets of the city, the
three of them, free spirits. Speaking of the majesty
that was Rome...

EXT. ROMAN FORUM RUINS - DAY

Great ruins of the heart of Rome. Triumphal arches, pagan temples, Corinthian pillars of strength and honor. Friedrich stands on the porch of an ancient ruined citadel, melodramatically expounding a lecture like a modern Socrates.

> NARRATOR (V.O.)
> ...And dreaming of its glory -- before it was
> destroyed by the "madness" of Christianity...

INT. COLOSSEUM - DAY

They glory from the stands over the open pits of the Colosseum. In their ears, the ghostly sounds of the masses thirsting for blood.

EXT. ITALY MOUNTAINS - DAY

The three of them hike through a forested area of a mountain, dressed more for the city than the country. Around them, breathtaking beauty.

Friedrich has a thought and pulls out his glasses and notebook to jot it down as they walk. He lags behind.

When he breaks out into the open. Before him is a majestic lake and a huge rock on the edge of the lake that juts upward from the earth. They stare up at it with awe.

> NARRATOR (V.O.)
> ...He discovered that each of them had separately
> dreamed of creating a university of learning,
> where free thinkers could grow in wisdom
> without the shackles of society and society's God.
> They began plans to make it a reality.

The two men stand before the large rock. Upon it, Lou gestures dramatically. A female Socrates.

The men look at each other with raised brows, impressed with this sassy young dilettante.

> NARRATOR (V.O.)
> ....The three of them had found perfect union, yet
> each with his own distinct opinion. It was an
> unholy trinity. Father, Son and Mother Goddess...

Rée stands by the lakeside looking out, thinking to himself. The water, a vast expanse before him.

Friedrich and Lou walk along the wood's edge talking. Now is Friedrich's opportunity. He pulls Lou aside into the woods to be alone. He gathers a heroic breath of courage.

>   LOU
> So you were that close to the Wagners?

Friedrich nods regretfully. She is entranced.

>   LOU
>   (lustfully)
> What is Richard Wagner like?

(beat)

> And Cosima? She must be -- beautiful.

>   FRIEDRICH
>   (sadly)
> She is...
>
>   (beat)
> They're not the only royal marriage in the world.

>   LOU
> I would love to meet them some day.
>
>   (dreamily)
> Bayreuth. Would you introduce me to them?

>   FRIEDRICH
> Lou, I must ask you something.

She awaits innocently.

>   FRIEDRICH
> Nobody reads my books now, but...

>   LOU
> They will, Friedrich. And when they do, all the
> world will tremble.

She's an actress, complete with vain excess. Friedrich is flattered. Confidence floods in.

FRIEDRICH

I know. And I want you to be there when it does.
By my side.

LOU

I will, Friedrich.

Friedrich's eyes light up with hope.

LOU

Paul and I will both be by your side.

FRIEDRICH

No. What I mean is...

And then, Rée enters the woods.

RÉE

Ho, you two! There you are! I thought I had lost
you to the spirits of the woods!

Lou looks at Friedrich, then back to Rée.

LOU

No. We were just discussing our "free union," our
"holy trinity."

RÉE

Did you discuss the problem of Elisabeth?

Lou looks at Friedrich, puzzled. He is embarrassed.

RÉE

Ah, yes, well. We must keep it a secret from the
Nietzsche family as long as possible. It seems
Friedrich is not quite as "free" of a spirit as we
were led to believe.

Lou looks back at Friedrich. She's waiting...

FRIEDRICH

It is one thing to brave the spite and scorn of
society's taboos. It is quite another to have to live
in the midst of such contempt.

> RÉE
> That's why we "immoralists" have to stick together. Family is the enemy.

> FRIEDRICH
> I have an idea.

Rée and Lou look at each other.

EXT. PHOTOGRAPHY STUDIO IN LUCERNE - DAY

Friedrich pulls Lou and Rée up to a store front.

INSET SIGN: "JULES BONNET: PHOTOGRAPHY"

Rée and Lou wonder what Friedrich is up to.

INT. PHOTOGRAPHY STUDIO - DAY

THE PHOTOGRAPHER, "artiste," prima donna pissant, stands next to his camera in frustrated impatience.

On the crude sweep stands a bewildered Rée. Behind him, a small wooden cart that Friedrich helps Lou step into. He guides her to kneel down in it.

Friedrich jumps away to a prop box a few feet away. He finds what he is looking for: a small whip. He brings it over to Lou. Hands it to her.

She affectionately raises the whip to shoo him away. He runs back to his position and the two men hold up the cart like a pair of oxen.

Lou shakes her head and raises the whip in mock anger. The picture SNAPS.

FREEZE FRAME ON THE INFAMOUS HOLY TRINITY PHOTO

EXT. THE LION OF LUCERNE SCULPTURE, LUCERNE - DAY

Friedrich sits with Rée at the famous sculpture in Lucerne. He is looking at the "holy trinity" picture.

> FRIEDRICH
> Paul, I want you to propose to Lou for me.

Rée is shocked.

> RÉE
> Friedrich. You just met her.

FRIEDRICH

I've never felt such elation, such total and complete oneness of being with anyone like this before.

RÉE

Well, I can't blame you for desiring her. She's rather... heavenly.

FRIEDRICH

Every Tristan has his Isolde. Every Antony, his Cleopatra.

RÉE

(sarcastic)
Every Macbeth, his Lady Macbeth.

FRIEDRICH

She's a goddess.

RÉE

Why don't you do it yourself?

FRIEDRICH

Nerves. I think I would vomit.

RÉE

So much for the "übermensch." But what about her freedom? Is marriage really necessary?

FRIEDRICH

Paul, I don't want to be alone. I want to be human again.

RÉE

And if she declines?

FRIEDRICH

Our plans for the university remain unhindered.

Rée looks at him, almost sadly.

RÉE

Very well.

Friedrich smiles widely.

>   FRIEDRICH
>   Thank you, my friend. Thank you.

Friedrich hugs him deeply. But Rée is a bit worried.

INT. HALLWAY SORRENTO RESIDENCE - DAY

Just outside the closed door of Lou's room we hear LOU'S AND RÉE'S VOICES
whispering.

>   LOU (O.S.)
>   He wants to marry me?! I knew it! Another man
>   begging for my hand!

>   RÉE (O.S.)
>   Sshhh. You don't want to be heard, do you?

>   LOU (O.S.)
>   How can I let him down? He's going to be
>   important someday, Paul. Dreadfully important.
>   And I want to be there when he ushers in the
>   revolution.

>   RÉE (O.S.)
>   Leave it up to me. I'll think of something.

>   LOU (O.S.)
>   You better. Oh, God.
>   (with increasing intensity)
>   Oh God. Oh God. Oh God! Oh God!!

This is far too melodramatic for her concern.

INT. LOU'S ROOM

That's because it's not her concern. It's her pleasure. Lou is having sex with Rée
on the couch. They're dressed. She's on top. Pins him precisely in place to
maximize her climax.

>   LOU
>   Oh God!!! Oh Goooood!!!!!

She flops down, exhausted.

> LOU
> Well, you better think of something fast, because I
> can't keep quiet for long.

She starts to attack Rée for more. He sighs with fatigue.

INT. FRIEDRICH'S ROOM SORRENTO RESIDENCE - NIGHT

Friedrich sits at his desk. Finishes his bottle of vodka. Flops back in his chair, a beaten man.

Rée sticks his head in the door and shocks Friedrich.

> FRIEDRICH
> Don't you knock, good man? What if Lou and I
> were in here making love?

Rée walks in ominously. He sees the empty bottle of vodka. Friedrich's glazed stupor.

> RÉE
> You're not supposed to be drinking.

> FRIEDRICH
> We humans, all too human. Bundles of
> contradictions, aren't we?

> RÉE
> Not all contradictions can kill you like that one
> can.

> FRIEDRICH
> Eat, drink and be merry, for tomorrow we die!

Rée sits down and Friedrich looks in his eyes. He knows already. He turns away in pain.

> FRIEDRICH
> She said no.

Rée gets up and comforts his friend with a hand on his shoulder.

> RÉE
> Friedrich, remember what you said.

Friedrich stops and looks at him.

FRIEDRICH

"The Son of Man betrayed with a kiss."

RÉE

Friedrich, she said she loved you...

(beat)

...but she's just not ready for marriage right now.

FRIEDRICH

She loves me?

RÉE

(trying to cover)

She'll consider it in a few years.

FRIEDRICH

I don't have a few years. But she said she loved
me?

RÉE

Well -- Platonically.

FRIEDRICH

Oh, yes! Platonic love! The great foundation of
Western civilization! Rational, sensible Greek love
of -- BULLSHIT!

Friedrich plops down, exhausted. Gropes at Rée's jacket.

FRIEDRICH

Where is that poison of yours?

Rée holds him off.

RÉE

Control yourself, Friedrich.

Friedrich pulls himself together in sad resignation.

FRIEDRICH

Control. Yes. I cannot give up control.

(sarcastically wags his finger)

I am -- the Author! The Master Storyteller!

>   (soberly)
> I've got a world to destroy and rebuild.

Friedrich winces in migraine pain, blacks out and falls on his bed.

Rée moves over. Stares down with deep regret. Friedrich stirs and mumbles.

> FRIEDRICH
> Cosima, Cosima. What did I ever do to deserve
> this?

Rée is touched by his friend's pathos.

INT. HALLWAY LOU'S ROOM - MORNING

Rée sneaks out of Lou's room, half-naked, carrying his clothes back to his own room.

Just missing him, Friedrich pounds gloriously down the hall to Lou's bedroom door, dressed in style.

He KNOCKS. Looks up and down the hall. Nothing. Lou opens the door, perturbed and naked underneath her open gown.

> LOU
> What?! Oh!

Friedrich is embarrassed. She pulls her gown closed.

> LOU
> Friedrich!

> FRIEDRICH
> Uh, Lou.

> LOU
> Come in. Come in.

> FRIEDRICH
> Well, I uh. Actually...

> LOU
> Friedrich, it's all right.

He does so sheepishly. And then gathers his courage.

> FRIEDRICH
> You had better start packing.

> LOU
> What do you mean?

> FRIEDRICH
> You said you wanted to be introduced to the
> Wagners, didn't you?

> LOU
> Yes.

> FRIEDRICH
> Well. I'm taking you to Tribschen. But don't tell
> Rée.

And Lou's confused gaze brightens into a childlike grin.

DISSOLVE TO:

EXT. TRIBSCHEN - DAY

A horse carriage pulls up to the mansion and Friedrich helps Lou out and onto the lawn. They walk over to a huge spreading weeping willow tree.

> LOU
> Oh, it's beautiful.

Friedrich smiles sadly. GRUNTS a half-hearted approval.

> LOU
> I have something for you.

She reaches into her pocket and pulls out a piece of paper. Friedrich is hopeful for any scrap of attention.

> LOU
> A poem I wrote. I wanted you to be the first to
> hear. It's called, "Prayer to Life."

She pauses for effect. Friedrich listens eagerly.

> LOU
> "Indeed, I love you life, as friend loves friend, in
> all your mystery --

Whether I wept or laughed again,
Whether you brought me joy or pain.
I love you even for the harm you do;
And if you must destroy me,
I'll tear myself away from you
As I would leave a friend.
To be for centuries! To live!
Wrap your arms about me once again:
If you have no more joy to give--
At least you still grant pain."

FRIEDRICH
That's beautiful, Lou.

LOU
Thank you.

FRIEDRICH
May I?

He takes the paper. Looks at it. Stuffs it in his jacket.

FRIEDRICH
I will score it, and have it read at my funeral.

She hits him playfully.

LOU
Oh, Friedrich, you're so morbid.

FRIEDRICH
I want to apologize for my cowardice.

LOU
No. You are not a coward. You are a hero.

FRIEDRICH
I should never have hid behind Rée to do what I
must do myself.

She gets nervous. He's starting again.

FRIEDRICH

Lou von Salomé, I want you to marry me. Be my
wife.

LOU
(affectionately)
Friedrich...

Friedrich searches for hope in her eyes. A sign. Anything.

LOU

...I'm flattered.

Just when it looks as if there may be some...

LOU

But there is so much I want to experience. I'm not
sure I ever want to marry.

Friedrich plummets.

FRIEDRICH

Paul said you might in the future.

LOU

He did?

She hides her anger.

FRIEDRICH

I'm sorry. I knew it! I'm spoiling our holy trinity.

LOU

No, no Friedrich. We can still be a holy trinity. We
just won't have any immaculate conceptions.

She smiles. Then Friedrich smiles. They LAUGH.

She kisses him on the cheek. Which embarrasses him. A nervous silence. Lou
breaks it.

LOU

Well, are you going to bring me inside?

FRIEDRICH

Oh, no. The Wagners aren't here.

> LOU
>
> Aren't here? You said you were going to introduce
> them to me.

> FRIEDRICH
>
> Tribschen -- is the lost spirit of Wagner. The
> carcass of a once great ideal.
>
> (looks longingly at the grounds)
> I'm going to have my sister take you to Bayreuth
> to meet them -- "in flesh and blood."

Lou looks at him delighted, then curious.

> LOU
>
> Oh, Friedrich!

She grabs him tight. Too tight for the poor love-sick wretch.

EXT. LEIPZIG TRAIN STATION - DAY

Elisabeth stands impatiently waiting. The TRAIN WHISTLE scares her. She just about has a fit, when...

Lou arrives with Friedrich carrying way too many bags for a normal human being. Elisabeth is shocked at the excess.

Lou runs to her. Hugs her gleefully. Elisabeth stiffens.

> LOU
>
> Oh, Elisabeth, Friedrich's told me so much of you!
> We'll be like sisters!

Elisabeth gives Friedrich the evil eye. He shrinks.

> ELISABETH
>
> He has? Well, he has not returned the favor to me,
> so I guess I have some catching up to do --
> "sister."

The WHISTLE BLOWS.

> TRAIN MAN
>
> All aboard for Bayreuth!

Lou hurries along. Friedrich follows with his burden.

Elisabeth slyly throws a bag on the already too heavy load. He GRUNTS. She gives him a wry look and saunters on.

> NARRATOR (V.O.)
> There is a concept in German folklore called, "doppelgänger." It refers to a ghostly counterpart...

EXT. BAYREUTH - DAY

The opera house juts into the sky with majesty. On its billboard: "PARSIFAL." Peasants walk about the streets.

> NARRATOR (V.O.)
> Someone so opposite of another that they reflect two sides of a single personality...

INT. LOU AND ELISABETH'S ROOM - DAY

Elisabeth chooses her evening clothes. Uptight in her Victorian corset and bustle.

Lou prances about in scanty underwear.

> NARRATOR (V.O.)
> To meet one's doppelgänger is a sign of imminent death.

> LOU
> Oh, aren't you excited to see the Wagners!

> ELISABETH
> (rolling her eyes)
> I am already well acquainted with their society.

A KNOCK at the door and Lou bounds to open it.

In strides PAUL VON JOUKOWSKY, flaming gay dress designer.

Elisabeth SHRIEKS and covers her already enshrouded body in horror. Lou leads him in.

> ELISABETH
> Who are you?!

> LOU
>
> This is the famous designer, Paul von Joukowsky.

Joukowsky carries his bag in and his ASSISTANT carries in a mannequin. Joukowsky smiles at Elisabeth, who backs up in horror into the next room and slams the door behind her.

> ELISABETH
>
> Insufferable!

Back in the room, Lou holds out her arms ready for styling.

> LOU
>
> Paul, make me a dress!

He grabs a measure tape and wraps it around her waist.

BACK ON ELISABETH'S SIDE

Elisabeth peeks out through the door. She sees Paul snuggling Lou and measuring her. She gasps. Shuts the door again. Looks to heaven.

> ELISABETH
>
> Lord, why me?

INT. BAYREUTH OPERAHOUSE - NIGHT

A scene from the third act of "Parsifal" plays out on stage. OPERATIC SINGING saturates the ears. On the cavernous stage, a splendorous garden flanked by huge castle walls. PARSIFAL the knight, young holy fool, is overcome at KUNDRY'S feet, the beautiful cunning seductress in wild abandon. She loves him as a god, as her redemption.

UP IN THE BALCONY

Lou and Elisabeth sit with Förster. Next to Lou, are TWO FAWNING MEN. She lifts a cigarette and both of them raise a match. She smiles.

Elisabeth is disgusted.

The Opera singing from PARSIFAL continues to play over the following visuals:

INT. WAGNER'S BAYREUTH HOME - NIGHT

A party at the Wagners. Richard and Cosima are with Lou, Elisabeth, and Förster.

Wagner kisses Elisabeth's hand. She smiles. Cosima smiles.

Richard, transfixed by Lou, grabs her hand and kisses it a bit too long and sensually.

Cosima hides her distaste. Elisabeth fumes with anger.

LATER -- AWAY BY THE CORNER

Elisabeth and Förster in a social circle of aristocrats.

Elisabeth fakes a smile. Looks over to see Lou with her own circle of men, gawking and vying for her attention. Elisabeth almost explodes. She pulls Förster aside.

OPERA MUSIC FADES DOWN

> ELISABETH
> That woman is a boorish outrage!

> FÖRSTER
> Lizzie.

> ELISABETH
> Libertine hussy!

> FÖRSTER
> Some women simply have -- personal magnetism.

Elisabeth looks up at him suspiciously.

> ELISABETH
> And are you under her spell of "personal magnetism"?

> FÖRSTER
> On the contrary, I'm already bewitched by a far more substantial sorceress.

He smiles slyly. Elisabeth blushes.

A snobbish aristocratic SOCIALITE interrupts them.

> SOCIALITE
> Excuse me. You wouldn't happen to be Elisabeth Nietzsche?

ELISABETH
(proudly)
I am.

SOCIALITE
My colleagues and I were wondering...
    (points to a group of smug Ivory
    Tower intellectuals)
Is your brother insane?

ELISABETH
(horrified)
Whatever are you talking about?

SOCIALITE
Your brother is an atheist, is he not?

Elisabeth looks to Förster for help.

SOCIALITE
Well. Is he an atheist because he is insane, or
insane because he is an atheist?

He smiles. The party of Intellectuals chuckle arrogantly. Elisabeth is outraged.

ELISABETH
How -- dare you!

FÖRSTER
Sir. Whoever you are, please go back under the
rock from which you slithered.

The Socialite glides back to his company of hyenas.

Förster draws Elisabeth close, protecting her.

FÖRSTER
That barbarism will be the death of the Fatherland,
yet.
    (beat)
Lizzie, remember when I told you about creating a
colony -- New Germany? Well, I've secured the
land deal in Paraguay. I have investors and a
group of daring pioneers.

> ELISABETH
> Oh, Bernhard, I'm so happy for you.

And then the ramifications hit her.

> ELISABETH
> When do you leave?

> FÖRSTER
> I can't leave. Not until I'm married.

Elisabeth looks at him in surprise.

DISTANT SHOT OF FÖRSTER AND ELISABETH

THE WAGNER OPERA SINGING RAISES AGAIN as Förster kneels before Elisabeth, her mouth wide, and pops the question. She breaks out bawling and nods her head vigorously. They embrace in sheer happiness.

INT. BAYREUTH FESTIVAL HOUSE - NIGHT

The final scene of "Parsifal" in the hall of the Holy Grail. Great pillars and arches. The roundtable. The altar of the Grail. Parsifal mounts the altar, takes hold of the Grail. Kneels in prayer. The Chalice glows, he's shrouded in light. The knights and squires sing of redemption. A dove descends. Kundry collapses, dead at Parsifal's feet.

INT. LOU'S AND ELISABETH'S BAYREUTH ROOM - NIGHT

Lou and Elisabeth get ready for bed, removing copious amounts of clothing, piece by piece.

Elisabeth hums to herself. Lou is happy for her.

> LOU
> Förster proposed to you tonight?

Elisabeth freezes in shock.

> ELISABETH
> How did you know?

> LOU
> It's written all over your face, woman. And all
> over the party this evening.

Elisabeth shudders in fear. Continues to unbutton.

> LOU
> Oh, don't worry. You were "decent" in your
> affections. It's just good to see you so -- happy.

As opposed to bitchy. Elisabeth softens a bit toward Lou.

> ELISABETH
> Please don't tell Friedrich.

> LOU
> Why not?

> ELISABETH
> I just -- I don't want him to be hurt.

> LOU
> Suit yourself.

> ELISABETH
> Lou?

Lou looks up from her undressing.

> ELISABETH
> Are you seducing my brother?

Lou looks at her bewildered, then stifles a laugh. Elisabeth doesn't follow.

> LOU
> I'm sorry. It's just that...

> ELISABETH
> What?

> LOU
> It is your brother doing the seducing.

> ELISABETH
> (scandalized)
> My brother is a saint and an ascetic!

> LOU
> He is neither.

ELISABETH

How dare you.

LOU

Fear not, Elisabeth. I'm uninterested in Fritz.

ELISABETH

You may fancy yourself a leech of famous men.
But you'll not tarnish the reputation of my brother
with your -- whorish instincts!

(beat)

And stop calling him Fritz!

LOU

Elisabeth, your puritanical vexation does me no
personal grievance. I am unconcerned about my
"reputation." Let others think what they will. And
as for your brother, He is the slave of his instincts,
not I. I could sleep in the same bed with -- Fritz --
and not suffer the slightest lustful desire.

Elisabeth pulls together her belongings in rage.

ELISABETH

My brother is making you! It's his image you're
feeding on!

LOU

His image all right. He wants to make me in his
image. Indoctrinate me with his ideas for his
pleasure.

(just realizing it)

Funny, isn't it. He doesn't believe in God. But he
surely acts like him.

ELISABETH

Stay away from my brother -- you -- you terrible
Russian!

Elisabeth gets to her door to leave.

LOU

Elisabeth.

Elisabeth stops.

LOU

Friedrich is a great man.
But I assure you, he is no deity.

Elisabeth SLAMS the door shut.

INT. NAUMBURG HOME - DAY

ANOTHER DOOR SLAMS SHUT. Elisabeth glares at a chastised Friedrich.

ELISABETH

I cannot believe it! First, you ruin your
relationship with Wagner, now this-- a ménage à
trois?!!

FRIEDRICH

Rée, Lou and I want to create new values together.
Damn society's conventions.

ELISABETH

Cohabitation with such a slut!

FRIEDRICH

But Wagner and Cosima...

ELISABETH

Wagner is different. Cosima was sacrificing to
genius.

FRIEDRICH

And what am I?

Elisabeth is caught by her words. But she regathers.

ELISABETH

If you could only have seen her flaunting her
indiscretion like a wanton -- harlot!

FRIEDRICH

Spare me your slave morality.

ELISABETH

It is one thing for free-thinkers to scorn social taboos in their private lives. It is another thing to do so in public!

FRIEDRICH

Is that all you care about, Elisabeth? Your status? Your "public" image?

She can't answer honestly.

ELISABETH

Can't you see what she is doing? She's using you. She wants to become famous through you!

FRIEDRICH

And what do you want, marrying this anti-Semite with his dreams of fascism?

ELISABETH

You're jealous. You're jealous because I'm actually doing what you've only talked about.

She has hit the nerve. Friedrich can't look at her.

FRIEDRICH

You're marrying him to spite me, aren't you?

ELISABETH

Spite?! I have spent my entire life in nothing but adoration and worship of you. And you reward me with this accusation of spite?!

Friedrich remains silent.

ELISABETH

If I were a good Catholic, I would join a convent and atone for your sins.

FRIEDRICH

You're not a good Catholic. You're not even a good Protestant.

ELISABETH

And you're not a good atheist.

Friedrich is surprised.

ELISABETH

That's right. You're a hypocrite. You scorn morality, but you cower in fear to let your family know.

Friedrich stands corrected.

ELISABETH

I tried to talk to Richard and Cosima to fix what you destroyed with them.

FRIEDRICH

I didn't ask you to fix anything! Stop trying to control my life!

(settles down disgusted)

You remind me of God.

Elisabeth looks deeply offended.

ELISABETH

I tried to help you find a wife, but your taste was for whores. I have tried to understand you and care for you despite our differences. But now, I finally know what your philosophy means. Your contempt for morality. --You hate God...

(beat)

...So you love evil.

She storms out of the room. Friedrich holds back.

INT. HALLWAY NIETZSCHE HOME

Franziska is in the hallway. She's overheard it all. Elisabeth makes eye contact with her and continues on.

Friedrich sees Franziska. She gathers her frail strength.

FRANZISKA

I want you to leave this house.

> FRIEDRICH
> Mother.

> FRANZISKA
> Why did you not tell me of this woman, Friedrich?

> FRIEDRICH
> Would you have me flaunt her in your face?

> FRANZISKA
> I do not understand these -- ideas of yours. But I
> know this: God is not mocked. You sow the wind,
> you reap the whirlwind.

> FRIEDRICH
> And what are you sowing by disowning me,
> mother?

> FRANZISKA
> You are a disgrace to your father's grave!

She hobbles out, leaving Friedrich utterly abandoned.

INT. FRIEDRICH'S ROOM

Friedrich sits down at his small desk. Pulls out an old, dusty Bible. Looks at it like he's going to read it. Opens it to reveal an envelope. Pulls the envelope out and leaves the Bible. In it is a bundle of deutschemarks. He puts them in his jacket and leaves.

> NARRATOR (V.O.)
> "In order to love one another, we must first hate
> each other. Thus saith Zarathustra."

EXT. NAUMBURG - DAY

It's a beautiful Autumn day. Leaves have not yet fallen, so the trees are like a child book fantasy of stunning colors. Birds float around.

Two young boys fish in the pond with eternity in their hearts.

EXT. RÖCKEN CHURCHYARD CEMETERY - DAY

Friedrich stands watching THREE WORKMEN use a pulley and tackle to carefully lower a large gravestone onto his father's grave.

Friedrich pays the CEMETERY MAN out of the envelope of money in his jacket.

The workers leave Friedrich alone as he leans in to read the large gravestone.

> NARRATOR (V.O.)
> Have you ever said Yes to a single joy? O my
> friends, then you said yes too to all woe. All things
> are entangled, ensnared. Love it eternally and
> evermore; For all joy wants eternity. Thus saith
> Zarathustra.

> INSET OF GRAVESTONE:
> Here reposes Karl Ludwig Nietzsche
> Pastor of Röcken.
> Born 11 October 1813 - Died 30 July 1849
> "Love never fails" - 1 Corinthians 13:8.

Friedrich lightly fingers the engraved words in thoughtful sadness. A few leaves flutter across the stone. Friedrich tears up.

> FRIEDRICH
> Father.

Tears of sadness turn to anger as Friedrich pounds the stone and breaks down into sobbing.

> FRIEDRICH
> Father! Why have you forsaken me?!

He looks up into the sky. But all around is SILENCE.

EXT. REE'S SORRENTO RESIDENCE - DUSK

Cold winter dusk. First snow flutters to the ground. A coach pulls up to the front of the residence.

Friedrich hauls baggage out of it and looks up at the beautiful manor.

> NARRATOR (V.O.)
> When we inquire after truth, are we seeking for
> rest, peace and happiness? What if the truth is
> ugly and repellent?

He trudges to the entranceway. Heaves the knocker. The door opens to a surprised Rée in his underwear, sucking on a pipe.

> RÉE
> Friedrich.

Friedrich smiles. Rée looks guiltily uncomfortable.

And then a giggling half-drunk Lou comes to the door. She's dressed only in her nightgown, open and revealing foreplay.

Her eyes lock with Friedrich's. She sobers. He backs up and stumbles down the steps in horror.

> RÉE
> Friedrich!

But Friedrich backs up into the coach. He throws his bags into the compartment.

> FRIEDRICH
> Back to the station!

The coachman shrugs his shoulders and gets ready to leave.

Rée doesn't know what to do. He finally runs out into the cold in his skivvies.

> RÉE
> Friedrich!

But it's too late. The coach door slams shut and rides away, leaving Rée in the street. Back at the door, Lou is bereft.

> FRIEDRICH (V.O.)
> And that, my dear Overbeck, is why the thought
> of suicide helps me through many a dreadful
> night.

INT. OVERBECK'S HOME - NIGHT

BACK TO THE PRESENT: 53-YEAR OLD Overbeck and wife Ida sit at the dinner table, just after dinner, with a bleary-eyed and worn 45-YEAR OLD Friedrich.

Friedrich finishes breaking off a piece of bread to eat from a loaf. Overbeck takes a sip of wine. Ida gets up to clean the dishes away.

> FRIEDRICH
>
> No one likes my work. I am a headache-plagued lunatic, crazed by too much solitude. And a half blind lunatic at that.
>
> (beat)
>
> I wanted to turn the world upside down, rewrite history. I can't even narrate my own story.

Friedrich looks wryly at Overbeck, then LAUGHS his head off. Overbeck follows suit.

Friedrich COUGHS. Waves for Overbeck to pass his wine glass. He does. Friedrich drinks deeply.

> FRIEDRICH
>
> You alone have remained a true friend through it all -- even when I wasn't.
>
> (beat)
>
> I should have made you my disciple.

Friedrich hands the wine back to Overbeck, who finishes it.

> FRIEDRICH
>
> Everyone else in my life has betrayed me. And I have betrayed everyone. My father is long dead. My sister has cheated me out of my greatest self-conquest. I am a victim of her merciless desire for vengeance. Wagner, an egomaniacal lunatic. Lou, a heartless manipulator. And Rée, a backbiting coward, and a candidate for suicide himself.

Friedrich looks at his friend.

> FRIEDRICH
>
> My only consolation is that Wagner is finally dead.

> OVERBECK
>
> I suspect all you have is -- your writing.

A look of revelation crosses Friedrich's broken face.

> FRIEDRICH
> That is all I have ever had. And I can only
> remember one period of pure ecstasy,
> unencumbered by torment...

EXT. MOUNTAIN LAKE - DAY

MEMORY FLASHBACK: Friedrich, NOW 39, sits all alone atop a huge rock at the edge of a vast lake, reading glasses on. He writes furiously on a tablet of paper.

This is the rock and lake that Friedrich had cavorted with Rée and Lou. Friedrich is on top of the world. Around him spins the sacred mountains and mythic forests. The sun pours through the clouds over the lake like a vision of supernatural wonder.

> FRIEDRICH (V.O.)
> Zarathustra. I wrote it in ten days. In memory of
> Lou. It was as if divinity rested upon me. Six
> thousand feet beyond humanity and time. I was
> the mere mouth, the medium of supernatural
> powers of revelation. A fifth gospel.

SFX: TIME LAPSE. The sun glides through the sky and sinks into the mountains. The moon rises. Friedrich watches. It's like a miraculous display of nature before the prophet.

EXT. LUTHERAN CHURCH - DAY

Well-wishers throw streamers and rice at a newly married Elisabeth, NOW 37, and Förster as they exit the church.

The NARRATOR's VOICE-OVER takes over from Friedrich's.

> NARRATOR (V.O.)
> "O Zarathustra, you philosopher's stone! You
> threw yourself up high, but every stone that is
> thrown must fall"...

Elisabeth and Förster pose for a camera shot, Elisabeth looks around the crowd.

There's Franziska, old and decrepit, but alive.

Cosima Wagner and two children, Isolde and Siegfried.

Franz and Ida Overbeck. Elisabeth, deeply wounded, next to an empty seat, where her brother should be. But is not.

EXT. SHIP SAILING WEST - NIGHT

Elisabeth leans on the rail, looking out to sea. Förster comforts her.

She follows him back into the cabin.

> NARRATOR (V.O.)
> ...O solitude, my home! Too long have I lived
> wildly in strange places not to return home to you
> in tears. To be forsaken, however is another
> matter...

EXT. SOUTH AMERICAN SEA PORT - DAY

The ship is docked at bay. SERVANTS carry crates and luggage down the gangplank.

A group of GERMAN PIONEERS crowd around Förster and Elisabeth. He grins into destiny. She is scared at the primitive state of it all.

> NARRATOR (V.O.)
> ...You higher men, learn this from me: The mob
> says, "Before God we are all equal, and all evil."
> But God has died: now we want the übermensch
> to live. Evil is man's best strength. Man must
> become better and more evil. Thus wrote
> Zarathustra.

EXT. SOUTH AMERICAN WEEDY PRAIRIE - DAY

A small contingent of carriages end their journey. Förster looks out the window and smiles. He hops out with Elisabeth.

He opens a large blueprint of detailed plans for the colony. Elisabeth smiles reluctantly but supportive.

The other pioneers get out of their carriages intrepidly.

INT. OVERBECK'S HOME - NIGHT

BACK TO THE PRESENT: Friedrich, 45, sits by the fire with Overbeck. Friedrich is wrapped up in blankets, sick and miserable. Overbeck sips tea and reads the newspaper.

> FRIEDRICH
> I'm reading Dostoyevsky. In "The Brothers
> Karamazov," Alyosha says if there is no God, then
> all things are permissible.

> OVERBECK
> (from the paper)
> Appalling.

> FRIEDRICH
> Sublime.

> OVERBECK
> (still reading)
> There's a fellow running around England killing
> prostitutes. They call him "the Ripper." He slashes
> their throats and spills their bowels.
> (winces)
> Truly sinister.

Friedrich's attention is riveted.

> FRIEDRICH
> But that's the point, Overbeck. There is no
> "sinister," no evil. Only wills in conflict. This
> "Ripper" lives beyond good and evil. Unhindered
> by the constraints of morality. Like Caesar,
> Napoleon. Zarathustra.

Overbeck gives him a weird look.

> FRIEDRICH
> He's overcome himself and society. He is the
> "übermensch."

> OVERBECK
> You're frightening me, Friedrich.

Friedrich smiles. Muses darkly.

> FRIEDRICH
> My life is now governed by the wish that things were not as I see them and that someone could prove me wrong.

> OVERBECK
> Prove yourself wrong.

> FRIEDRICH
> It's too late, I am stuck within the vortex of my own ideas. Sucking me in. Pulling me toward the inevitable. Apocalypse.

Overbeck stares at his comrade, trying to understand.

> NARRATOR (V.O.)
> Because there is nothing beyond good and evil. A man becomes more of one -- or the other.

> OVERBECK
> So it's out of your control?

> FRIEDRICH
> I am the crucified. I am Dionysus.

Overbeck hands a letter to Friedrich out of the pile of mail.

> OVERBECK
> A letter from your sister.

Surprised, Friedrich opens it and reads hungrily.

> ELISABETH (V.O.)
> Dearest brother, I felt it proper to write you as some time has passed and hopefully feelings have calmed.

EXT. FÖRSTERHOF, NEW GERMANY - DAY

Elisabeth, NOW 43, writes on a piece of scrap paper in the hot South American sun. Bugs BUZZ around her head. Dirty sweat.

> ELISABETH (V.O.)
> I am writing you from our established colony,
> Försterrode of New Germany. It is like Paradise
> here. A beautiful land of milk and honey.

She looks out onto the open expanse of drudgery. Swats another fly. The sun boils her skin.

Down the way, a colonist gets stuck in swampy mud carrying a bucket over his shoulder.

> ELISABETH (V.O.)
> ...The colonists are a bit extravagant as they all live
> in luxurious built homes...

A FAR SHOT of the pathetic little bungalow huts, falling apart. She's lying. Or rather, telling her own narrative.

> ELISABETH (V.O.)
> ...served by the most innocent and pure of
> natives...

A colonist runs out of one of the huts, beating a Spanish slave with a branch.

> ELISABETH (V.O.)
> ...We have a surplus of cattle and farm animals...

A handful of sickly dying cows pasture in a broken down fenced in area.

> ELISABETH (V.O.)
> ...And so far, our capital growth far exceeds our
> expenditures...

INT. FÖRSTERHOF - DAY

Förster sits in desperation at his desk in their small hut. He writes on an accounting sheet and picks up a mere few Deutschmarks. Swipes everything to the floor in frustration.

> ELISABETH (V.O.)
> ...In the evening, we sit on our porch and watch
> the beautiful sun set over the river and fields of
> grain...

INT. FÖRSTERHOF BEDROOM - NIGHT

Elisabeth busts open the door to see Förster drunk out of his gourd on the bed. He throws up all over himself.

She grabs the bottle and storms out the door.

> ELISABETH (V.O.)
> ...We too struggle with the daily things of life, but all in all, it's a wonderful New Germany. Please write. I am still your sister.

EXT. FÖRSTERHOF PORCH - NIGHT

Elisabeth sits crying her eyes out on a chair on the porch.

INT. OVERBECK'S HOME - NIGHT

Back to Friedrich and Overbeck. Friedrich closes the letter.

> OVERBECK
> Don't kill the bearer of bad tidings.

They share a moment of connection. But then Friedrich doubles over in pain.

Overbeck helplessly comforts him.

> FRIEDRICH
> I'm all right. I need to return to Turin.

> OVERBECK
> Friedrich, you're not well.

But he knows he cannot stop him. Friedrich looks at him. His only friend in the world.

> OVERBECK
> Friend, you're always welcome back.

EXT. STREETS OF TURIN - NIGHT

> SUPER: Turin, Italy - 1889

Friedrich walks through empty streets. Pulls his cloak tighter in the cold winter chill. Stumbles. Keeps going.

A GROUP OF CAROLERS sing THE HALLELUJAH CHORUS at a street corner. Passersby murmur "Merry Christmas" to each other.

Friedrich ignores them all. Then he sees a HORSEMAN with his carriage, beating his horse mercilessly.

> HORSEMAN
> You stupid beast!

Friedrich runs across the street.

Catches the man's hand before he can whip again. Glares into the man's soul, eyes ablaze.

He throws the Horseman to the ground. Turns to the horse and throws himself on the horse's neck. Holds on, weeping desperately.

P.O.V. FROM ABOVE

Friedrich falls to the ground. Tries to rip off his coat.

Falls flat on his back, arms spread wide in the snow. It's like he's crucified to the ground, GASPING for breath.

The Carolers come near to help.

> NARRATOR (V.O.)
> I recognize my destiny, he said at last. I am ready.
> My final loneliness has begun...

EXT. JENA ASYLUM - DAY

A cold dead winter's day. The asylum is a godforsaken edifice, crumbling and forgotten. Very far from the grand natural scenery of Friedrich's entire life.

> NARRATOR (V.O.)
> A God now dances in me. Thus saith Zarathustra.

INT. JENA ASYLUM - DAY

A wreck of an institution before hygiene regulations. CRAZY MUMBLING PSYCHOTICS wander around.

Overbeck walks warily through the dirty hallways, led by a bespectacled white-jacketed arrogant Freudian-looking WARDEN.

> WARDEN
>
> We don't follow the superstition of demons
> causing insanity and such. We are very modern
> and scientific. We use hypnosis, cocaine and
> electrical shock therapy. Believe me. This lunatic
> asylum is Friedrich's hope for curing his soul.

A SHARP FEMALE SCREAM from a distant therapy room dissuades Overbeck from believing him.

Then they hear the sound of PIANO PLAYING wafting from the room they enter.

> NARRATOR (V.O.)
>
> And Zarathustra said, "It is not madness but
> health that is the symptom of degeneration,
> decline, and the final stage of culture."

INT. ASYLUM WARDEN'S OFFICE - DAY

Inside the Warden's office, Friedrich plays at a piano in the corner. A DOCTOR watching him stands out of the way.

> WARDEN
>
> Friedrich. Someone's here to see you.

Friedrich stops playing. Whispers harshly to the Warden.

> FRIEDRICH
>
> Ssshhh! Can't you hear? You're interrupting the
> narrator of my grand tragedy!

It's as if Friedrich can actually hear what no one else in the story can: The Narrator's Voice-over.

The Warden just looks sadly at the confused Overbeck.

Friedrich listens around him for more narration.

> FRIEDRICH
>
> Go on.
>
> > (beat)
>
> GO ON!

But there is nothing. So Friedrich plays on. It's operatic. It's Lou's poem.

> FRIEDRICH

I love you even for the harm you do;

And if you must destroy me,

I'll tear myself away from you

As I would leave a friend.

He hums the rest of the words. Overbeck steps up to him.

> OVERBECK

Is that Wagner?

> FRIEDRICH
> (shaking his head)

It's a love song to my wife, Cosima.

Overbeck is sad at the remark. The Warden whispers.

> WARDEN

He thinks he's Wagner?

Then Friedrich's playing stops. He holds his head in pain. Pounds on the keys like a maniac.

> FRIEDRICH

He who hates me, hates my father!! He who hates

me, hates my father!!

The Doctor runs over to him, joined by THREE INTERNS, who hold him down from hurting himself. Friedrich whimpers.

INT. ASYLUM, FRIEDRICH'S BED - NIGHT

Overbeck sits beside Friedrich's bed sadly looking out the window at the moon. Friedrich is in a delirious stupor, sweating and mumbling.

All of a sudden, Friedrich's eyes pop open.

> FRIEDRICH

Overbeck.

His eyes, aware. A moment of clarity, he's all there. Overbeck slides closer. Friedrich struggles through his physical misery to speak.

> FRIEDRICH

Overbeck, I've seen it.

OVERBECK

Seen what, Friedrich?

FRIEDRICH

The abyss. I've looked into the face of absolute
void...

    (beat, he smiles)
...And it has looked into me.

OVERBECK

You're not well.

FRIEDRICH

I've gone too far to turn back. I can't turn back. I
must preach this gospel to all creation.

Overbeck watches his fallen comrade with pain.

FRIEDRICH

Where is Elisabeth?

OVERBECK

Still in Paraguay.

FRIEDRICH

It's just as well. I'm having all anti-Semites shot.

    (beat)
Where is my father?

Overbeck stares sadly at Friedrich, unable to tell him the truth, unable to see him
relive the pain all over again.

FRIEDRICH

No man comes to my father, but through me. I am
the way, the truth and the life. I am Dionysus, the
Crucified!

Friedrich's eyes glaze over. He falls back into delirium.

NARRATOR (V.O.)

O Zarathustra, You said in your heart, "I will
ascend to heaven; and I will make myself like the

Most High." How you have fallen from heaven, O
Son of the morning.

> FRIEDRICH
> (blurting out)
> I'm not fallen from heaven! I am the übermensch!

Overbeck is shocked by Friedrich's screaming out to no one. And we see again:
It's as if, in his insane state of mind, Friedrich can actually hear the Narrator and
is responding to him.

As Friedrich falls back into a mindless rocking, Overbeck reluctantly leaves the
room, giving one last look at his friend, who softly hums Lou's poem over the
following visual:

EXT. SWISS LANDSCAPE - TIME LAPSE

The vast Swiss Alps thrust up into the heavens amidst a TIME LAPSE of
beautiful clouds flowing overhead

INT. FRIEDRICH'S ROOM, JENA ASYLUM - NIGHT

Friedrich sits painfully curled up in the corner of his cinderblock room cell,
sniffling and shivering, still HUMMING.

> NARRATOR (V.O.)
> My hand has done this. I capture the wise in their
> own deceit. I inflict pain and give relief.

Friedrich stops. Then, as if replying to the Narrator...

> FRIEDRICH
> Vindictive coward.

Or is he just blurting out random thoughts that by chance appear to create a
dialogue?

> NARRATOR (V.O.)
> I deprive the leaders of the earth of their reason
> and make them wander in a pathless waste.

> FRIEDRICH
> Self-righteous bigot.

> NARRATOR (V.O.)
> Friedrich, I am the Lord your God.

> FRIEDRICH
> Possessive tyrant.

> NARRATOR (V.O.)
> You shall have no Gods before me.

> FRIEDRICH
> Jealous bastard.

> NARRATOR (V.O.)
> I have given and I have taken away. Thus saith the
> Lord.

> FRIEDRICH
> Then I prefer hell.
> (defiantly slow)
> Thus - saith - ZARATHUSTRA!

Friedrich goes back to HUMMING his opera song. And the identity of the Narrator has finally been revealed: HE IS GOD HIMSELF -- telling the tragedy of history's most infamous atheist.

INT. OVERBECK'S HOME - NIGHT

Overbeck sits reading the newspaper, HUMMING Friedrich's previous opera rendition.

His wife Ida, knits, but keeps looking at him with concern. Overbeck stops humming. The clock's TICKING penetrates the silence.

Overbeck crunches up his paper. He can't read. Ida bleeds for him.

> IDA
> How long has it been?

A long guilty pause.

> OVERBECK
> Too long.

EXT. JENA ASYLUM - DAY

Overbeck helps a frail Franziska up the walk to the Asylum. She's 64 now but looking 80.

INT. ASYLUM PLAYROOM - DAY

The Warden leads Overbeck and Franziska through the door. Inside is every mental disorder known to man. Some patients nervously twitching. Others, stoically robotic. A playroom of pathetic wretches.

Overbeck and Franziska look around.

> OVERBECK
>> Where is he?

The Warden shrugs. Franziska zeros in on an inmate squatting in the corner, rocking in delirium, mumbling to himself.

She starts for the corner, but Overbeck takes the lead. He reaches the inmate and turns him around.

It's Friedrich. He's dirty and clearly uncared for. He looks up at Overbeck.

> FRIEDRICH
>> It is my wife, Cosima, who has brought me here!
>> And my father who left me!

Overbeck is shocked. Franziska, heartbroken. Friedrich pulls away and returns to his rocking.

> FRIEDRICH
>> I am stupid because I am dead. I am dead because
>> I am stupid. I am stupid because I am dead. I am
>> dead because I am stupid.

Franziska receives a gust of courage, pushes Overbeck aside and grabs Friedrich by the arm with a gentleness only a mother could have for her child.

> FRANZISKA
>> This is no place for my son!

She pulls him along triumphantly. Overbeck is humiliated. The Warden doesn't know what to do.

INT. NAUMBURG HOME - DAY

SUPER: Weingarten 18, Naumburg, Germany

Franziska feeds Friedrich with a bib on him. He glares out into the distance.

EXT. NAUMBURG COUNTRYSIDE - DAY

Franziska pushes Friedrich in a wheelchair down a walking path.

INT. NAUMBURG HOME - NIGHT

Friedrich is tucked away in bed. Franziska reads to him from the Bible. He does not listen.

> FRANZISKA
> "The Lord is my shepherd, I shall not want. He
> maketh me to lie down in green pastures; He
> leadeth me beside the still waters... "

INT. FÖRSTERHOF NEW GERMANY - DAY

Elisabeth walks into the room with desk and papers. It's a mess. She picks up the cash box. Empty.

She looks over at TWO POLICE OFFICIALS and a BANKER holding a contract.

> FRANZISKA (V.O.)
> "...He restoreth my soul; He leadeth me in the
> paths of righteousness for His name's sake..."

EXT. HOTEL DEL LAGO, PARAGUAY - DAY

Establishing shot of the hotel. South Americans all over the place. A normal day.

INT. HOTEL DEL LAGO ROOM - DAY

Förster finishes a bottle of wine and throws it to the floor with a CRASH. He reaches into a sack and pulls out a gun. He holds out a contract and rips it to shreds. He slowly puts the gun to his temple.

The mirror in the corner sprays with blood.

> FRANZISKA (V.O.)
> "...Yea, though I walk through the valley of the
> shadow of death, I will fear no evil; for Thou art
> with me: thy rod and thy staff comfort me..."

INT. CORONER'S OFFICE - DAY

A SEEDY LITTLE CORONER pulls the sheet over Förster's grimacing dead face. He turns to Elisabeth, who hands him a wad of money.

He turns to the table and writes on the death certificate: "HEART ATTACK." Elisabeth is satisfied.

> FRANZISKA (V.O.)
> "...Thou preparest a table before me in the
> presence of mine enemies: thou anointest my head
> with oil; my cup runneth over..."

EXT. FÖRSTERRODE NEW GERMANY - DAY

Elisabeth gazes at the slum of a colony in regret. She gets in the carriage with her luggage and it drives away. She is dressed in black as she will always be from now on.

EXT. SHIP BACK TO GERMANY - NIGHT

Elisabeth stands at the railing deep in thought and pain.

> FRANZISKA (V.O.)
> "...Surely goodness and mercy shall follow me all
> the days of my life: and I will dwell in the house of
> the Lord forever."

INT. FRIEDRICH'S BEDROOM - DAY

Franziska finishes reading the Psalm and looks at her son with beading tears.

> FRANZISKA
> Lord have mercy on my son.

And then Franziska's image DISSOLVES INTO ELISABETH sitting in the chair in her signature black. She closes the Bible and sets it on the table. Her pity wells up within.

>ELISABETH
>Oh, Fritz. Where are they now? "The Unique" is
>getting rich off her husband's legacy. That terrible
>Russian is tramping around Europe. Mother is
>dead. The Master is dead. Rée is dead.
>>(beat)
>They have all left you. But I am here.
>I will never leave you nor forsake you.
>>(beat)
>I've been reading your books, Fritz. I'm beginning
>to understand you now. The pain of your genius.
>Your greatness.

Friedrich continues his oblivious gaze. She tucks his blanket in tighter.

Then pulls out the crucifix from so long ago and puts it around Friedrich's neck.

She trims the lamp and leaves the room. Friedrich stares out the window to the bright FULL MOON.

EXT. NAUMBURG HOME - NIGHT

That same full moon shines upon a row of horses tied to a post.

One of them bucks restlessly. In his eyes, the wildness of desire. His body, a slave.

EXT. NIETZSCHE ARCHIVES, NAUMBURG - DAY

Overbeck, 64 AGAIN, watches a storefront lined with people waiting to get in.

On the doorpost: "WEINGARTEN 18 - NIETZSCHE ARCHIVES."

Elisabeth, 54 AGAIN, steps out to address the crowd.

>ELISABETH
>Please! Please, you'll have to have patience! We
>are limited in space. I assure you I want every one
>of you to see the new display of my brother's
>original manuscripts!

Then her eyes meet Overbeck's. A moment frozen in time.

INT. NIETZSCHE ARCHIVES OFFICE - DAY

Overbeck stands before Elisabeth in her office. She sits at a large desk. He is furious.

> OVERBECK
>
> I will not.

Elisabeth glares at him silently.

> ELISABETH
>
> Then I will use legal redress to force you.

Overbeck turns distraught before her calm malevolence.

> ELISABETH
>
> My brother's correspondence with you is a part of
> his estate. Of which I am the executor. I will have
> them.

He walks around the bookcases and grandeur of the office, filled with pictures of
Friedrich and Elisabeth, Elisabeth in New Germany with Förster, and of course,
just Elisabeth.

> OVERBECK
>
> How did you get your mother to sign away her
> rights?

> ELISABETH
>
> My mother is dead.

> OVERBECK
>
> You threatened to have her declared incompetent!

> ELISABETH
>
> Ah, but I didn't put her into a lunatic asylum, as
> you did my brother.

Overbeck is humbled by his mistake.

> ELISABETH
>
> What exactly are you hiding, Herr Overbeck?

> OVERBECK
>
> Did you ever consider I may be protecting you?

Elisabeth stiffens with shock.

ELISABETH
Well, then, I'm sure the Nietzsche Archives are the
safest place for them.
(beat)
I believe you have something else for me as well.

Overbeck reaches into his leather case and pulls out the manuscript he had stolen earlier, "ANTICHRIST."

He reluctantly hands it to her. She smiles victoriously.

ELISABETH
You'll be glad to know I've decided to publish it --
eventually.
(beat)
I'm having a hard time keeping up with the
demand for his books. They're selling more than
ever.

OVERBECK
This is not right.

ELISABETH
Right? This is not right?
(beat)
You are an atheist, are you not, Herr Overbeck?

Overbeck is afraid to admit it.

OVERBECK
Elisabeth, please.

ELISABETH
Then tell me, if you believe there is no God, then
what exactly is "right?"

Overbeck is silenced. Elisabeth picks up a book on the desk and reads.

ELISABETH
Nothing is "right." "Everything is false. Nothing is
true. All is permitted."
(beat)
Might makes right.

She slams the book shut and looks at Overbeck.

> ELISABETH
> Thus saith Zarathustra.

Overbeck picks up the book and looks at it. The book cover reads: "THE WILL TO POWER," by Friedrich Nietzsche.

> OVERBECK
> What is this?

> ELISABETH
> It's Fritz's last work. I'm editing it from his notes.

> OVERBECK
> He never started that book. He spoke of it, but I know he never wanted it published.

> ELISABETH
> Herr Overbeck, you are not privy to everything in my brother's life. You are not God.

> OVERBECK
> And neither are you.

This offends her.

> OVERBECK
> You wanted to control your brother's life and now you want to control his legacy.

> ELISABETH
> My brother and I had a bond that you will never understand. You turned him against me.
> (beat)
> This meeting is over. You'll receive a warrant for the procurement of any and all Nietzsche correspondence which legally and properly belongs in the care of the Nietzsche Archives. Good day, Herr Overbeck.

Overbeck is overcome by dark realization. He leaves.

For a moment, Elisabeth is bothered, but then she reaches down and pulls out a letter written to "DEAR MOTHER."

She finishes scratching out "Mother" and writes in "Elisabeth."

EXT. NIETZSCHE ARCHIVES - DAY

Overbeck steps out into the cold winter day and covers up.

The NIETZSCHE ARCHIVE sign hangs over him like a dark cloud. The crowd, still hungry for a sight of their "scriptures."

> OVERBECK
> I'm sorry, dear friend.

He unhooks his horse and rides off.

EXT. HILLSIDE CHURCH - DAY

Up on the hillside, by the church, a loose horse wanders. It rears up, neighs and runs off, wild and free.

INT. RÖCKEN LUTHERAN CHURCH - DAY

A funeral is in progress. It is Friedrich's. He finally lays in peace in his casket.

At the front of the sanctuary, a SINGER sings the haunting melody of Lou's "Prayer to Life."

> SINGER
> "Indeed, I love you life, as friend loves friend, in
> all your mystery--
> Whether I wept or laughed again,
> Whether you brought me joy or pain..."

In the crowd is Elisabeth, face barely visible through her shrouded covering.

Across the aisle, Overbeck glares at her.

And there's Cosima too, now age 50 and still beautiful. Siegfried and Isolde, both in their 20s, sit beside her.

> SINGER (O.S.)
> ..."I love you even for the harm you do;
> And if you must destroy me,

I'll tear myself away from you
As I would leave a friend..."

Friedrich's casket is closed. Six PALL BEARERS, including Overbeck, pick it up and carry it down the aisle past Elisabeth who can barely watch it.

> SINGER (O.S.)
> "To be for centuries! To live!
> Wrap your arms about me once again:
> If you have no more joy to give--
> At least you still grant pain."

EXT. RÖCKEN CHURCHYARD CEMETERY - DAY

> SUPER: August 28, 1900

It's a cold and dreary winter day. Skeletal trees, barren land. Very much the opposite of the beautiful panoramas which we have seen throughout the story.

> FRIEDRICH (V.O.)
> Dearest Lisbeth. Promise me that when I die, only
> my friends shall stand about my coffin - no
> inquisitive crowd...

A huge throng of people surround the churchyard and push in.

> FRIEDRICH (V.O.)
> ...See that no priest or anyone else utters
> falsehoods at my grave side, when I can no longer
> defend myself. And let me descend into my tomb,
> an honest pagan.

The casket is lowered into the grave hole. A large silver crucifix adorns the casket.

A LUTHERAN PRIEST utters his rites. The opposite of everything Friedrich asked for.

Overbeck watches it all with sadness and resolve.

Elisabeth steps up with melodrama.

> ELISABETH
> I would like to read a poem that my brother wrote
> to me.

(she pulls out a paper)
"The tie that binds sister to brother
Is strongest of all ties I hold;
They're riveted to one another
more firmly than ties of gold."

She's crying now. And so do other women in the crowd. In her hand, she clutches the crucifix passed between them.

Overbeck seethes with rage at Elisabeth's gall. Now, Friedrich's VOICE-OVER...

> FRIEDRICH (V.O.)
> I have a terrible fear that one day, I shall be
> pronounced holy.

An old, GAUNT MAN in a black overcoat and hat steps up behind Overbeck. He looks like the angel of death. SOMEONE in the crowd speaks up.

> SOMEONE
> Friedrich Nietzsche! Hallowed be thy name to all
> future generations!

SFX: As Overbeck stands there, the crowd of mourners DISSOLVES AWAY to night. Overbeck is alone at the grave.

Next to Friedrich's grave in this churchyard cemetery is his father's large gravestone from earlier.

The Gaunt Man steps up to Overbeck like a ghost and whispers in his ear. He has the VOICE OF THE NARRATOR.

> NARRATOR
> Nietzsche fought against God. But you -- you are,
> by far, more guilty. You have found a way -- to
> tolerate him.

And he's gone. A CRANE SHOT shows the now lone figure of Overbeck against the church and the cold, stark landscape of the hillside.

INT. OVERBECK'S HOME STUDY - DAY

Overbeck crashes open the door to his study. It's lined with bookcases and messy paper piles.

He runs up to his desk and hurls papers to the floor with a wild swipe.

140

Grabs a pile of books and launches them at a bookcase in rage. Rips paper from his typewriter.

> OVERBECK
> Words! Words!! Words!!!!

He looks up at the bookcase. With a heave ho, pulls the thing to the ground. Books spill to the floor.

He looks up to see the worried face of Ida at the door.

He breaks to his knees in sobbing tears. Ida comforts him.

> IDA
> There, there.

> OVERBECK
> I will never write another page again.

> IDA
> Why?

> OVERBECK
> Because I am a hypocrite.

She doesn't follow.

> OVERBECK
> My entire academic career has been a lie. I deny God, and yet... I affirm him with every word I write.

> IDA
> You're only human.

> OVERBECK
> All too human.

He sighs. Sits down on the bookcase. Ida listens patiently.

> OVERBECK
> I've been trying to figure out why Nietzsche went insane. And of all the possible explanations, to me it seems quite possible that he did not bring madness into life with him, but that it was the consequence of his own ideas.

Overbeck is dark with self-revelation.

BLACK AND WHITE 1930'S NEWSREEL FOOTAGE:

EXT. NIETZSCHE ARCHIVES - DAY

1938. A large procession of Nazi vehicles pull up to line the street outside the Archives.

Elisabeth, 92 years-old, stands at the door with pride as ADOLPH HITLER approaches her with his entourage and hands her a dozen roses. They pose for the cameras.

> FRIEDRICH (V.O.)
> I know my fate. One day, my name will be
> associated with the memory of something
> frightful...

INT. NIETZSCHE ARCHIVES - DAY

NEWSREEL FOOTAGE: Hitler and Elisabeth are now looking at pictures on the wall. Elisabeth hands Hitler the book "The Will to Power." He smiles and shows it to the cameras.

Elisabeth backs up a bit and Hitler moves closer to a bust of Friedrich. He stands a few feet away in respect, posing for the cameras.

FREEZE FRAME on the infamous photo.

> FRIEDRICH (V.O.)
> ...a crisis without equal on the earth, the most
> profound collision of conscience. A decision that
> was conjured up against everything that had been
> believed, demanded, hallowed so far. I am no man...
> > (beat)
> I am a fatality.
> > (beat)
> I am dynamite.

:CUT TO BLACK

THE END

Postscript:
The Themes Behind "Nietzsche: A Dangerous Life"

Friedrich Nietzsche. Perhaps no philosopher has been more controversial, more debated or more misunderstood than this scandalous German from humble Lutheran beginnings, who rose through personal adversity to defy the conventions of Victorian society as well as the foundations of Western Civilization itself: Christianity. And perhaps no philosopher's story could be more relevant in today's post-modern world. *Nietzsche: A Dangerous Life* is the story of a free-spirited "free-thinker" whose ideas would change the world but would carry with them dark and unintended consequences on himself, on those around him and on future generations.

Nietzsche's Worldview

With his ideas of Perspectivalism, the "Death of God," the Will to Power and others, Nietzsche attempted to destroy Christianity and replace it with a new reality for a new kind of man who would create a new morality and overcome not only traditional thought forms, but man himself. This proposed "Overman" would be scandalized by his surrounding culture for his rejection of its norms, but would ultimately be the hero of the next generation, a man before his time, a prophet not accepted in his home town.

And Nietzsche saw himself as this "Overman," this voice of one crying in the wilderness that the old belief system based on the Christian God is dead and a new one must begin, one based on the utter rejection of absolute truth, absolute morals and objective reality. For it is in the positing of these absolutes that he thought man and society became slaves of the will to power of weaker men who use those absolutes to control others through guilt and manipulation.

God, being the ultimate absolute, is therefore the ultimate guilt manipulator.

In a way, Nietzsche knew his ideas would not be immediately accepted, indeed that he would be scorned and persecuted. But he took on the task with resolute daring and boldness, dreaming of a new millennium when he would be looked back upon as the heroic harbinger of a new and great society. It was a dangerous risk, but an inevitable one, and necessary to his thinking.

Unfortunately, this denial of absolutes and objective reality creates a dilemma for the philosopher and his new post-modern society of "heroic" Overmen without moral restraint. And that dilemma is irrationality and self-contradiction. To say that there is *no* objective reality is itself an objective proposition about reality. To propose that there are *no* absolutes, is itself an absolute proposition. To say that traditional morality *ought not* be imposed on others is itself a moral imposition on others. And to deny the existence of God is to deny the very foundation of rationality itself, which is a necessary prerequisite for the philosopher to even engage in the act of "denying" in the first place. In short, his beliefs refuted themselves, leaving him in a precarious and vulnerable state of irony and self-contradiction.

And it is this ironic contradiction that marks Nietzsche's beliefs as particularly distinct in the history of philosophy. He is a philosopher who rejects philosophy. A moralist who rejects morality. A writer who rejects language, grammar and rationality. A man who believes there is something fundamentally wrong with those who believe in fundamental right and wrong. But can a man believe such things without it affecting his personal life? Can he think such contradictory thoughts without suffering beneath the weight of such mental tension? Quite simply, no. Our contradictory thoughts eventually work themselves out into our lives in the same way that a computer program will eventually reveal its contradictions in programming embedded deep within its lines of code.

A Theme of Contradiction and Irony

And it is in this context that *Nietzsche: A Dangerous Life* takes on its subject matter. A thematic context of the irony and contradictions in human nature. Our propensity to self-deception. We say one thing, but we often live another. We reject society's conventions, yet we cannot seem to extricate ourselves from it. We hide our true feelings from fear of rejection or reprisal. We are, in short, hypocrites.

But the story does not address this dilemma from a dry exposition of the man's philosophy. Rather, it does so from an investigation of his stormy relationship with his dear sister, Elisabeth, an admiring devoted sibling with her own contradictions. In a way, their love/hate relationship embodied the very struggle inherent in Nietzsche's own worldview. A struggle of wrenching one's self free from the ties that bind, whether they be familial, societal or religious. And that "freedom" brings with it its own bondage. Loneliness, isolation and despair are just a few examples of the internal agony that comes from killing a part of yourself, be it right or wrong, good or bad.

Coming from a strong Lutheran family background, both siblings began with a deep religious impulse. Friedrich's troubles begin when his father, a Lutheran minister, dies and Friedrich cannot forgive God for taking from him the one man he most worshiped and adored. By the time he comes home from college, his anger with God is consummated in his adoption of atheism and the painful tug of war begins with his sister, who cannot understand her brother's rejection of her cherished religion. But her devotion to him remains steadfast despite this gaping hole of separation, thus marking the beginning of a love/hate relationship of self-deception that would last their entire lives

And there are many other contradictions that wage war in Friedrich's life. His complete disdain for the "barbaric" Victorian values, yet his inability to stand up to his family. His rejection of vanity and aristocracy, yet his misery at being rejected by those very same people. His detestation for his sister's religion and anti-semitism, yet his inability to extricate himself from her. His free-spirited denunciation of conventional morality, yet his impotence at communicating his forbidden love for Wagner's wife. Not to mention his very conventional infatuation with the libertine feminist Lou von Salomé. He is a man who snubs traditional values of true love and then drowns in the loneliness and despair that results from never finding that true love.

Elisabeth's Contradictions

To make matters more complicated, Elisabeth has her own contradictions she refuses to face up to. She typifies the Victorian conventions of vanity concealed behind etiquette. She desires to be a part of the aristocratic echelons of society, and she'll use anyone she can to do so, even her brother. She loves her brother, but uses him for her personal gain. She worships him, but castigates him for his irreligion. She believes that life is meaningful yet lives a petty life herself. By the end of the story, in the name of honoring her brother, she creates his legacy for her own personal gain. While she is deeply devoted, her religion is actually a shallow foundation of cultural heritage which she readily casts aside at the end of her life to embrace the national socialism of her beloved Führer. And the ultimate irony of all is that while she maintains her convictions, she adopts her brother's beliefs and becomes the very "Overman" he proposed. One who creates her own reality and ends up recreating him in her own image.

And so the man who proposed that there are no absolutes and that we must create our own becomes a victim of his own beliefs. And his beliefs then become the rallying point for the evil terror of Nazism. A terror he would decry with all that is in his soul, but could not refute because his own beliefs logically lead to it. If there are no absolutes and no morality that men are beholden to, then the will to power is the only justifier and might makes right. The Nazi's simply defied society's conventions and created their own reality. They were truly the Overmen that Nietzsche proposed. They could not have twisted Nietzsche's beliefs because there is no truth to twist according to Nietzsche. Truth is what the strong determine.

And in 1937, the Nazis were the strong.

So even though Nietzsche may have abhorred nihilism and the evils of genocide, he has no moral authority to complain, because his beliefs inevitably lead to and logically justify it all. As Dostoevsky pointed out in his *Brothers Karamazov,* if there is no God, then all evil is permissible because ultimately there is no "evil."

Overbeck's Contradictions

To keep *Nietzsche: A Dangerous Life* from becoming a dreary depressing funeral of human folly, the character Franz Overbeck is introduced. His presence brings hope and light into an otherwise dark tale. Because Friedrich goes insane, it would be difficult to tell his story through his own eyes of breakdown, so the story is told instead from the perspective of the academic Overbeck, Friedrich's only lifelong friend and confidant. As Friedrich's foil and reflection, Overbeck's own struggle of contradiction within his soul mirrors Friedrich's, yet provides the opportunity for redemption missed in Friedrich's and Elisabeth's own lives. Friedrich is the passionate radical who wants to change the world. To the contrary, Overbeck is the calm rational man who wants a quiet unobtrusive life. He is amused with Friedrich's youthful zeal but finds in him a heroic and zestful experience of life missing in his own.

Overbeck's' contradictions lie in his unwillingness to risk his comfort by revealing his unbelief in his surrounding religious culture. The man is an atheist teaching the New Testament at a Christian University! He justifies his contradiction by seeing himself as a "subversive" but he really is just afraid of the consequences of going against the grain, the risk to his own comfort and reputation.

As he sees Friedrich's life unfold, or rather, unravel, Overbeck comes to realize that he himself is the ultimate hypocrite of all. Overbeck's refusal to reveal his true beliefs is cowardice compared to Friedrich's bravery. As a ghost of his own conscience whispers to him at Friedrich's grave, "Nietzsche fought against God. But you -- you are, by far, more insidious. You have found a way to tolerate him." In one sense, if there is no God, if God is truly "dead," then all of Overbeck's propriety is a facade for a meaningless universe. And the world around him, a world enmeshed in religious belief, is not merely wrong, but a colossal fraud demanding a prophet's reaction of denunciation—that is, the life Friedrich himself lived.

But in a deeper and truer sense, Overbeck discovers the biggest fraud of all is his own atheism. As he turns over his bookcase in frustration at the end of the story and decides to never write again, he tells his wife that he is the ultimate hypocrite because he denies God yet affirms him with every word he writes. Not only is he an atheist teaching religion, but if atheism is true, if there is no ultimate meaning to the universe, then words, indeed language itself, has no meaning. Nietzsche once wrote, "I am afraid we are not rid of God because we still have faith in grammar." His writing reduces to the rambling gibberish of an insane mind. Interestingly, this pressure of a contradictory lifestyle and the ceasing of writing bears itself out in Overbeck's real life letters and biography.

This revelation of self-deception is for Overbeck the first step toward redemption and reconciliation with the God he ran from all his life; The God that Wagner turned to at the end of his life; the God that Elisabeth lived a mockery of hypocrisy before.

The Birth of a Tragedy

And so *Nietzsche: A Dangerous Life* is a tragedy. Friedrich is a hero because he dares to defy the morality and reasoning of the prevailing culture. But he is a tragic hero who is done in by his own flaws. He goes too far and defies the very foundation of morality and rationality all together, resulting in an unresolvable philosophical, psychological and spiritual tension.

Friedrich is a man who fights against God and society and loses. Not so much because his enemies fight back but because his own ideas self-destruct and backfire against him. He suffers from the unseen, unintended consequences of his own ideas, because ideas have consequences.

The Point of it All

Ideas have consequences. That's the ultimate premise of Nietzsche: *A Dangerous Life.* While many people believe that philosophy is for armchair academics in their ivory towers, with little relevance to "everyday life," they are severely mistaken. What a person believes about the world will ultimately affect not only his behavior, but his psychological and even physical welfare. The contradictions in those beliefs will manifest themselves in a contradictory lifestyle of the kind displayed in each of the characters in *Nietzsche: A Dangerous Life.*

There are several theories about the cause of Friedrich Nietzsche's insanity. And true to the thematic tension of contradiction, all of them are given voice in the story. From Friedrich's implied excursion into prostitution, resulting in syphilitic symptoms, to his father's genetically transmitted sickness and headaches.

But the most intriguing and controversial of all origins, and the one proposed in this story, is the one considered by Overbeck (also found in his actual letters):

That Friedrich so fully embraced his belief in perspectival reality, and the utter negation of meaningfulness and rationality, that the contradictions inherent within his philosophy overcame him. He finally reconciled the tensions in his philosophy by fully embracing all the contradictions, and in so doing, fully incarnating irrationality.

Insanity is the logical end of full and consistent living out of the belief in an absurd universe without meaning. Denying God is denying the very foundation of all rationality. To deny the foundation of rationality is to leave one's self with nothing but irrationality. Absurdity. Insanity. Atheism is philosophical insanity. Living out that philosophy with absolute consistency can only result in actual insanity. And the reason why we do not have a world of committed lunatics is *self-deception*: Man's singularly unique ability to convince himself of a lie, and to live hypocritically so as to avoid the implications of that lie. Perhaps after all, Nietzsche faced the lie and embraced it in its fullness.

Conclusion

Herein lies the relevance for today of *Nietzsche: A Dangerous Life*. Perhaps *we* are the beginnings of that society that Nietzsche dreamed of. Our post-modern rejection of absolute truth and embracing of moral relativity and subjective experience can be found in the common expressions of "do your own thing," "create your own reality," "don't impose your morals on me," "what's true for you is not true for me," and many others. Western society has degenerated into a cacophony of trivialized special interest groups, attempting to assert their wills to power over the majority. Modern tribal warfare.

Deconstructionism revises all literature, indeed all history, into a mish mash of subjective relative meaningless interpretations. There are no absolutes: no absolute truth, no absolute morality, no meaning to anything that exists other than the meaning we as individuals import into it. Claims of truth are merely interpretations. There is only power. All human relations in this view reduce to power. Therefore all morality and theories of knowledge merely service the pursuit of that power. Convenient ideas for someone who wants to justify their own immorality or desire to control others.

Nietzsche proposed these ideas a hundred years ago, and they are only now coming into vogue, making him both the grandfather and prophet of our post-modern world, a world that has seen the most extensive destruction of lives through the tyrannical will to power of godless rulers the world has ever known. The guillotines, gulags, gas ovens, killing fields, "cultural" and "proletariat" revolutions of the 20th century have all destroyed untold millions of lives in the name of "the death of God," making the religious crusades and inquisitions of the previous two thousand years look like a drop in the bucket of man's inhumanity to man.

Is this post-modern relativity desirable? Do we really want the results of such thinking? Do we really want to embrace the philosophy that unwittingly justifies the abominations of tyranny and genocide? For without absolutes, we can none of us complain when our neighbor rapes our wife, steals our money and enslaves our children, for all there is, is the will to power, all there is, is the rule of the strong over the weak without any moral obligations on the strong.

And God help you if you are the weak.

God help us all.

More Screenplays as Literature

The Last Knight
An Historical Epic Movie Script About the Siege of Malta in 1565

Home Movies
A Family Comedy Movie Script About Time Travel and Family Dysfunction

Nietzsche: A Dangerous Life
An Historical Biography Movie Script About History's Most Infamous Atheist

John Brown's Body
An Historical Epic Movie Script About the Man Who Started the Civil War

Alleged
An Historical Drama Movie Script About the Infamous Scopes Monkey Trial

Death Before Dying
An Action Thriller Movie Script About a Hero Fighting Modern Day Pirates

Pressure Point
An Action Thriller Movie Script About Environmentalism and Corporate Murder

Descent of the Gods
A Horror Movie Script About a Reality TV Show and Alien Abduction

Double Life
A Psychological Noir Thriller Movie Script About Virtual Reality and Obsession

Noah Primeval: The Movie
An Epic Fantasy Movie Script About the Ancient World Before the Flood

A. D. 70
An Historical Epic Movie Script About the Fall of Ancient Jerusalem

Before I Wake
A Psychological Crime Thriller Movie Script About a Cop Who Can See Through the Eyes of a Killer

Cruel Logic
A Psychological Crime Thriller Movie Script About God's Existence and the Consequences of Ideas

To End All Wars
An Historical WWII Drama About Allied Soldiers in a Japanese Prison Camp

I receive commissions from links to Amazon books above.

Sign Up to Get Brian Godawa's Updates, Movie Reviews, Other Scripts & Books.

www.Godawa.com

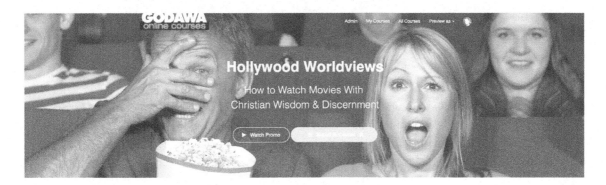

Get 25% OFF the Informative Hollywood Worldviews Online Course

Limited Time Offer

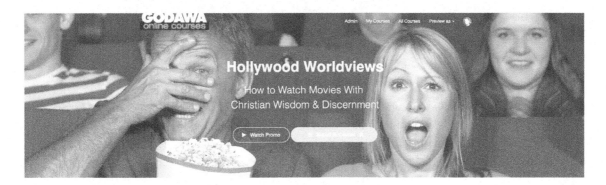

How to Watch Films with Wisdom and Discernment
Amazing Video Lectures with Powerpoint and Film Clips!

Brian Godawa, Hollywood screenwriter and best-selling novelist, explores the power of storytelling in movies and in the Bible.

You will learn how storytelling incarnates meaning, worldview and redemption in movies.

You will discover the nature of subversion, and how narratives compete and win in the culture wars of both movies and the Bible.

You'll receive a Biblical foundation for understanding sex, violence and profanity in movies and storytelling.

And a whole lot more! Click the link below to see everything you will get.

The regular price is $139. You'll get 25% off if you use the coupon below. You'll pay just $104.25.

Use this Coupon Code to get 25% Off: SAL2525

https://godawa.com/hwc/

Book Series by Brian Godawa

See www.Godawa.com for more information on other books by Brian Godawa.

Chronicles of the Nephilim

Chronicles of the Nephilim is a saga that charts the rise and fall of the Nephilim giants of Genesis 6 and their place in the evil plans of the fallen angelic Sons of God called, "The Watchers." The story starts in the days of Enoch and continues on through the Bible until the arrival of the Messiah, Jesus. The prelude to Chronicles of the Apocalypse. ChroniclesOfTheNephilim.com (paid link)

Chronicles of the Watchers

Chronicles of the Watchers is a series that charts the influence of spiritual territorial powers over the course of human history. The kingdoms of man in service to the gods of the nations at war. Based on ancient historical and mythological research. ChroniclesOfTheWatchers.com (paid link)

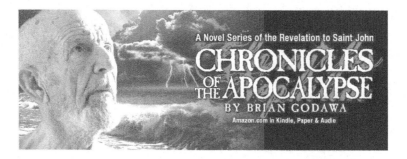

Chronicles of the Apocalypse

Chronicles of the Apocalypse is an origin story of the most controversial book of the Bible: Revelation. An historical conspiracy thriller trilogy in first century Rome set against the backdrop of explosive spiritual warfare of Satan and his demonic Watchers. ChroniclesOfTheApocalypse.com (paid link).

About the Author

Brian Godawa is the screenwriter for the award-winning feature film, To End All Wars, starring Kiefer Sutherland. It was awarded the Commander in Chief Medal of Service, Honor and Pride by the Veterans of Foreign Wars, won the first Heartland Film Festival by storm, and showcased the Cannes Film Festival Cinema for Peace.

He also co-wrote Alleged, starring Brian Dennehy as Clarence Darrow and Fred Thompson as William Jennings Bryan. He previously adapted to film the best-selling supernatural thriller novel The Visitation by author Frank Peretti for Ralph Winter (X-Men, Wolverine), and wrote and directed Wall of Separation, a PBS documentary, and Lines That Divide, a documentary on stem cell research.

Mr. Godawa's scripts have won multiple awards in respected screenplay competitions, and his articles on movies and philosophy have been published around the world. He has traveled around the United States teaching on movies, worldviews, and culture to colleges, churches and community groups.

His popular book, Hollywood Worldviews: Watching Films with Wisdom and Discernment (InterVarsity Press) is used as a textbook in schools around the country. His novel series, the saga Chronicles of the Nephilim is in the Top 10 of Biblical Fiction on Amazon and is an imaginative retelling of the primeval history of Genesis, the secret plan of the fallen Watchers, and the War of the Seed of the Serpent with the Seed of Eve. The sequel series, Chronicles of the Apocalypse tells the story of the Apostle John's book of Revelation, and Chronicles of the Watchers recounts true history through the Watcher paradigm.

Find out more about his other books, lecture tapes and dvds for sale at his website www.godawa.com.

BLANK PAGE

BLANK PAGE

BLANK PAGE

BLANK PAGE

BLANK PAGE

BLANK PAGE

BLANK PAGE

Made in United States
Orlando, FL
16 June 2022